Advance Praise for Houses of Healing

"I found *Houses of Healing* to be powerful, insightful and realistic. If used seriously, it can move many prisoners from a viewpoint of feeling hapless, hopeless and helpless toward responsibly examining and actively choosing values that will guide their lives toward being self-respecting and helpful human beings."
> — Dr. Donald Cochran, Commissioner of Probation,
> Commonwealth of Massachusetts

"*Houses of Healing: A Prisoner's Guide to Inner Power and Freedom* is an excellent product — a positive resource for prisoners. It should be particularly helpful for long-term prisoners who have reached a reflective phase in their incarceration."
> — Perry Johnson, Immediate Past President,
> American Correctional Association

"*Houses of Healing* is a book written for inmates whose message is for all of us, whether we are locked up in prisons of bricks and bars or ones we have created ourselves."
> — Joseph D. Lehman, Commissioner of Corrections,
> State of Maine

"The 5 billion spent to build prisons represents 5 billion dollars worth of lost opportunity.... unless prisons become HOUSES OF HEALING. This book reflects the author's understanding of the tremendous human potential lying dormant in our prisons. A must for anyone who wants to change."
> — Dot Walsh, Violence Prevention Coordinator,
> STEP, Inc., Boston, Massachusetts,
> and Middlesex County House of Correcrtions

HOUSES *of* HEALING

A Prisoner's Guide to Inner Power and Freedom

Robin Casarjian

LIONHEART PRESS

Library of Congress Catalog Card Number: 94-73682
ISBN 0-9644933-0-6

First Edition published 1995 by
The Lionheart Foundation
(20,000 copies)

Second Edition published 1996
(15,000 copies)

Third Edition published 2001
(30,000 copies)

Fourth Edition published 2007
(20,000 copies)

Fifth Edition published 2008
(15,000 copies)

The Lionheart Foundation
Box 194 Back Bay
Boston, MA 02117

Casarjian, Robin.
Houses of Healing:
A Prisoner's Guide to Inner Power and Healing

Printed in the United States of America

Editors: Jan Johnson, Betsy West, Naomi Raiselle
Proofreading: Suzanne Roger

Design: Dan Mishkind/Impress, Inc.
Design Assistant: Jeff Potter

Cover Illustration: Linda Bleck
Photo Enhancement: Luke Jaeger

Table of Contents

INTRODUCTION

MY PRISON WORK started in 1988 when I was invited to give a few presentations on the subject of forgiveness. At the time I was writing a book on forgiveness, a subject I had lectured on for many years. One of my first prison talks was at the Massachusetts Correctional Institution (MCI)-Gardner, a medium security prison for men. When I spoke with the psychologist who coordinated the program, he said that he would post some flyers around the prison announcing the upcoming talk. But, he warned me, because my lecture was not being offered as part of an ongoing group, he didn't know if many men would attend.

As I drove down the highway the morning of the talk, I wondered if more than a few men would voluntarily show up for a talk on forgiveness. At that time the population at MCI-Gardner was 700. When I arrived at the room where the talk was to be held, 120 men were waiting for me to begin.

I was deeply moved by the response of the group; by the thoughtful questions they asked, by the insightful comments they made, by their desire and willingness to share their own experiences with me and with each other. I was surprised by the large number of people who stayed around after the presentation, eager to learn more.

I was so moved and uplifted by the response that by the end of my visit that day, I knew that I wanted to continue to work with prisoners around the difficult and challenging issues of anger, guilt, remorse, shame, forgiveness of others, and the essence of emotional healing, forgiveness of oneself. I was sure that many prisoners would welcome the chance to use time in prison as an opportunity to heal if they were offered direction and encouragement.

Since that first day, I've offered presentations to hundreds of men and women in prison, and led numerous 7 to 15-session courses entitled "Emotional Awareness/Emotional Healing." I've also facilitated a year-long group for lifers and long-termers. The Emotional Awareness/Emotional Healing course has served as an important turning point for many. As one inmate said, "This course has given me a new outlook and a new direction. It has been a transforming light in a darkening world."

Not everyone who signed up for the course did so because they thought they would benefit from it. One man came up to me after an introductory talk and said, "I'm going to sign up for your group just to prove you're wrong." I told him he was welcome to attend. All I asked was that he bring some openness. By the last session he was sorry to see the course end. It had helped him cope with prison life. He felt much more in control. His ulcers stopped acting up. His relationship with his wife and children became kinder and more honest. He began to find comfort in a spiritual life that he had lost touch with for years.

For those who were ready, the course offered guidance on how to manage stress and transform some of the anger and frustration that is innate to prison life. For the first time, many of the participants found the safety and direction to start recognizing and healing the emotional wounds that fueled their addiction, violence, and criminal behavior. They had an opportunity to learn to care more for themselves and others and to feel more in control of their lives. Many began to connect with a deeper spiritual reality.

As a result of the enthusiastic response to the courses, I created the Lionheart Prison Project (now called "The National Emotional Literacy Project for Prisoners"). The goal of the project is to share as much of the spirit and content of the Emotional Awareness/ Emotional Healing course with as many inmates as possible. I have attempted to capture the essence of the course — respect, encouragement, new teachings and ideas, practical "hands on" exercises, questions for reflection and self-exploration — in the following pages. The goal of the Project is to distribute eight to fifty copies of this book, in English and in Spanish, free of charge, to every prison in the United States.

Is This Book for You?

Houses of Healing: A Prisoner's Guide to Inner Power and Healing is for anyone who is interested. Clearly some people in prison, like some outside of prison, want little or nothing to do with personal growth or emotional and spiritual healing. Some people aren't interested in this inner work. Some aren't ready for it. Yet after teaching in the prisons for more than seven years now, I have seen that more and more people want the guidance and direction to help them use their incarceration productively. Some women and men aren't actively looking for emotional and spiritual healing, but when the guidance to do the work actually becomes available to them, they choose it. We can't choose what we don't yet know exists.

Perhaps you've been looking for some way to make sense out of your pain and suffering. Perhaps you simply want some relief. As Joe, a participant in one of the classes said, "This work has opened up the door that I had been so desparately trying to reach and open myself." I feel confident that if you are open to what you find here, prison can be a "house of healing" for you. You *will* find some relief. And, like Joe, you will increasingly discover the true meaning of greater power and freedom.

Perhaps you've already been using your time to heal, seeking emotional and spiritual growth in recovery programs like AA or NA; in a prison ministry; or in individual or group counseling. If, like many people doing time, you are already on a path of healing, I hope this book will serve to further support and inspire you. I'm glad you are choosing to read it.

Maybe you haven't ever read anything like this before. Perhaps boredom or curiosity drew you to pick this book up. If you read through these pages and participate in the exercises, I think you will discover your curiosity has served you well. Welcome to a new adventure!

I find that many people in prison don't seek support or healing because they don't feel good enough about themselves to even try. Troy, a young inmate, said "When I first looked into this class I didn't think that I was worth trying to better myself. I have never really liked who I was and how I led my life." People who feel bad about themselves often feel like they don't deserve a decent life. They feel like they're not worth investing any effort in. In truth, we *all* deserve to heal and feel better about who we are. In case you feel this way, I want you to know without a doubt that *you are worth the effort.* You do deserve to have a life that is more positive, hopeful, and loving than the one you've had.

If you shy away from reading and learning something new because learning has been difficult or discouraging in the past, it is important to realize that learning does not depend on what grade you completed in school or your past success. It depends on your willingness to learn now. You *can* learn — if you are willing to have some patience with yourself along the way.

Many people don't invest any positive energy in themselves because of a profound sense of resignation. They have a belief that it's not worth trying because no matter what they do, life won't ever get any better. As Julio wrote, "I've always tried to find a source I could begin to address why I was guilt-ridden, afraid of loving, and why these kinds of feelings were causing me to literally lock myself up into a pattern of drugs, jail, and denying myself to mature. Before this course I had resigned myself into being worthless because I had always run from responsibility and had been a druggie so long I thought it was all I would ever be. But now I've found a way of dealing with feelings that were doing me harm.... Life is going to be worth living again." If, as you read this, you are feeling resigned to having a life that looks like it's always looked and feels like it's always felt, know a better life is possible. Life *can* change for the better. Even if a part of your mind is saying "that's not true" or "this person doesn't know what she's talking about," I say to you as Julio said to me, *life can be worth living again!*

If you are incarcerated, I hope this book will guide and inspire you. Rather than letting yourself be emotionally deadened and depressed by your prison experience, you can use this time to wake up to your true self, to a depth of personal power and self-respect the likes of which you may not have known before. Then you will be able to appreciate what your past has to teach you, without defining yourself solely in terms of your past actions or personal history. You'll see new options and move on knowing that you can have a happier, more satisfying life. As difficult as the prison experience can be, I know that prison can be transformed into a house of healing for you. I've seen it happen many times before. I've seen it happen for people who didn't imagine that their lives could be different.

In addition to guiding and inspiring, I hope this book will serve to dispel some of the prejudice and stereotypes about incarcerated men and women. In this country, the media portrays — and the public perceives — most prisoners as all being pretty much the same. Prejudice against prisoners, like any other prejudice, means we see people whom we pre-judge as static and unchanging. We decide they are horrible or stupid or no good, or whatever. And then that's the way they are! When we see through a filter of prejudice, we don't see people-in-process. Prisoners, like everyone else on this earth, are in the process of changing. They are in the process of becoming more wounded, or they are in the process of growing, learning, healing.

When we look beyond our pre-judgments and see the potential for growth and healing in others, we have to let go of our static images and assume a more responsible attitude to the way we treat that person or group. Seeing prisoners as people-in-process challenges us as a society to respond to prisoners in a more humane and intelligent way. Quite honestly, some of the most thoughtful, mature, compassionate people I have ever met are people in prison doing life and long-term sentences. Many have murdered. They committed their crimes many years ago and have used their time to grapple with their actions, the impact of their actions, their feelings, and their profound and appropriate guilt and remorse. Out of a difficult past they have re-created themselves as humans of great depth and compassion.

There is a healthy potential and creative power in you that we need in our society. But first you probably need to be guided, as we all need to be guided, beyond the psychic prison of misguided judgments, limiting self-definitions, and closed hearts. Only then will you (or anyone) be able to recognize and choose positive, constructive, healing options.

I am confident that if you bring some patience, openness, and courage to the thoughts and self-reflective exercises in this book, you will find that prison can and will be a "house of healing" for you. The experience of inner power and freedom are your option and your right to claim.

Some Suggestions for Using This Book

As you read through the following pages you will notice that in addition to the general text there are a variety of self-reflective exercises. When you come to one of these sections, rather than reading at your usual pace, take some time to reflect on them.

The sections set off by the directions to "Pause and Reflect" are usually a series of questions to ask yourself. You may answer them in your mind, or you may find it helpful to write your answers down.

From time to time you will see "seed thoughts." These are thoughts that are boxed and set in bold print. Seed thoughts are ideas that can serve to inpsire new insight and awareness. You are encouraged to write each seed thought on a piece of paper, and carry it with you or put it in a place where you will see it often. Whenever you notice it, pause for a few moments and think about its meaning.

There are also longer exercises and visualizations. Before you read them get comfortable and then allow yourself to freely imagine the scenes that are described.

If you find yourself excited by this book you might want to share it with others. You could start a small support group, reading the book, discussing the concepts, and sharing your experiences if you want to. Or, you may want to introduce this book and some of the ideas and exercises that follow to a support group you're already in. Another great way to share the ideas in this book is by reading it out loud to someone with difficulty reading.

Throughout this book you will find many first hand accounts by prisoners. As you read their writing, I ask you to keep in mind that most of them were written by average prisoners who chose to participate in my classes. Their writing offers an intimate visit into the lives of the people who have led the way. These are people who have not allowed personal pain, peer pressure, societal numbness, and the darkness of fear to stop the light from shining in. They offer a look at the healing of individuals who have committed crimes but who didn't let their past stop them from transforming their lives. Their personal stories bring us into lives where greater personal peace and dignity have been restored.

To Readers On The Outside

Although this book is written primarily for men and women who are actually in prison, to varying degrees we are all prisoners of our own limiting beliefs and fears. As the title of prison educator Bo Lozoff's book aptly reads, *We're All Doing Time*. The issues of personal healing are certainly not limited to the prison population. Because we're all doing time — whether you are a family member or a friend of a prisoner, a prison volunteer, a prison employee, or anyone else — I hope the guidance in this book will be useful for you. We have all been locked out of our own hearts for far too long now, held captive by our fear and lack of love. The following pages can serve as a guide to help free us so we can find our way back into our hearts. And in the true spirit of healing, discover the desire to take others with us.

* * *

Note to all readers:

I wish to express one regret to all readers but especially to incarcerated women. Although I have taught in the one women's prison in the state where I live, the opportunities for working with women have been limited. As a result, in the pages that follow there are far fewer personal accounts by women than I would have liked.

PART 1

CHAPTER I

Doing Time

"There's no better time to realize that you're not a failure in life.
You've just been delayed."

— Victor

REGARDLESS OF WHAT you have done or how long you have been
or will be in prison, you're not a failure unless failure is what you
accept for yourself. In fact, it's impossible to be a failure if you use
your time well.

If you've been in for awhile you know there are many ways to use
your time well — continuing your education on your own; if a
program is available, working toward a GED or college degree;
participating in group counseling; attending groups like AA or NA;
participating in job skills training; volunteering in programs like
those for the elderly or youth-at-risk that the prison may offer the
community; or getting involved with a prison ministry. You can
work on developing and maintaining positive family ties and nurturing positive friendships. You can be a good friend to fellow
inmates. By practicing stress-reducing techniques like relaxation
and meditation you can support your emotional and spiritual well-
being. You can also expand your knowledge and self-understanding
by reading certain books and articles. You probably know of others.
The essence of all time well spent is that it helps you experience the
peace, dignity, and positive potential of your own true nature.

One of the greatest dangers that confronts any prisoner is not using time in prison consciously and, as a result, getting used by it. That amounts to finding oneself six months, or five years, or twenty years later with an inner life that repeats over and over and over with the same old craving, anxiety, hostility, anger, and self-doubt. By using your time well you break out of this inner prison. You learn how to "do" your time. You make the most of it. As one inmate wrote, "Time is precious. Learn how to do your time. Don't let time run you. Stop. Listen. Hear the knock. If you can't hear it then turn the radio or T.V. off."

I have met many inmates who felt that nothing short of being in prison would have been dramatic enough to break the cycle of thinking and acting that robbed them of a chance at really living — of experiencing any real peace, inner power and freedom. Ironically, in a place where the freedom and power to make a hundred practical decisions a day is routinely stripped away, you *can* discover the true meaning of freedom and power. No matter what is going on around you, you can experience some control over your own destiny. You can experience a power and freedom that *cannot* be taken away.

Joe Before incarceration I was living my life like a lot of the men in failing communities. I was living on a day-to-day basis. Hustling, stealing and carrying on in a life without a cause or purpose. No world existed outside of the environment where I lived. There were no hopes of a better future. There were no great memories of yesterday. There was only living, with "survival of the fittest" as the everyday mentality. How was I to change at this stage in my life? I found it extremely difficult. In fact, I believed that I couldn't change. I was just another human being that had been used to living the lifestyle that so many in my community had been living. I had no idea of there ever being alternatives that I could choose from. The only thing I seemed to care about was keeping my macho image and fitting in. I thought my life would end up the same as many others that I've known — dead or in prison.

I now look at those times as one chapter closing in my life and a new chapter beginning. Because I was taken from my environment that I had been so accustomed to, I was forced to face change. I resisted change as much as I possibly could, and resistance brought nothing but exhaustion and misery. Change was all I had left and I decided not to let my life end at that point. When I became more open-minded, a whole new world opened up right before my eyes. What I came to find out was that you are capable of change and personal healing no matter how bad off you think you are.

Crisis to Opportunity

The English word "crisis" means "a time of great danger or trouble." The Chinese word for "crisis" means both "danger *and* opportunity," a different and more hopeful perspective.

Going to prison is a crisis for most everyone. It is often the outer manifestation of months, years, or even a lifetime of inner turmoil and crisis. It is most often the outer manifestation of confinement in an inner prison of fear, powerlessness, hopelessness, guilt, shame, anger, and low self-esteem.

The men and women who participated in the Emotional Awareness/Emotional Healing course are no exceptions:

Bob's father was an alcoholic. He put Bob down every chance he got. His mother, who was terrified of his father, never protected him. Bob went into the Army and served one year in Vietnam. When he returned, he got a job with the telephone company. Despite a life that looked fine from the outside, Bob felt down and depressed. "To ease the pain and boredom," as he said, he started doing cocaine. To support his increasing habit, he got involved in selling. He was arrested, tried, and given ten years.

Jim's father left when he was two years old. He didn't hear from him again until he was twelve. His young mother was left to raise four boys on her own. Until he was fourteen, James managed to do pretty well in school. He was good-looking and well liked. At fifteen he joined a gang and stopped listening to his mother. At seventeen he became a father. At seventeen he killed a girlfriend's old boyfriend because he didn't like what the guy was saying. He's in with a life sentence.

Raul's parents were both alcholics. His father left when he was five. His mother couldn't handle the responsibility of parenting. He and his sister were separated and put into foster homes. He lived with four different families. Starting at age six, he was sexually abused by a foster mother and father. The abuse stopped when he was taken out of that home at age nine. At age fourteen, he started sexually abusing children who were six to nine years old. At twenty-two he was arrested for sexually abusing children in his neigborhood. He's in for nine years.

Steve and his two sisters were raised by both parents. His parents were cold and controlling. There was little love or affection in the family. He did really well in school and went to college for a few years. He dropped out and started to work his way up in a major corporation. He became obsessed with having more money and living in the fast lane. It was the only thing that made him feel "good". He embezzled over $300,000 from company accounts. He's now doing three to five years.

Cindy was raised by her grandmother. She was sexually abused by her uncle from age eight to thirteen. At sixteen she became a drug addict and a prostitute. By nineteen she had a daughter of her own. She moved from one abusive relationship to another. At twenty, Cindy was arrested for selling crack cocaine. She's in for twelve years. She's now HIV-positive.

Crisis becomes so woven into the fabric of many peoples lives that by the time they reach adulthood, crisis is sometimes all they have known. Many seek relief from this reality through drugs and alcohol, further clouding the picture. Statistics indicate that 66% of people entering prison are alchohol or drug abusers. Every addict's life is in perpetual crisis. There is no balance. No rest. No clear perspective.

But crisis, no matter how bad it is, can be an opportunity, a positive turning point in the course of one's life.

Time in prison can be, in it's own very strange way, a gift. Incarceration offers an opportunity to step back from "life as usual" — to be sober and face life directly, to re-evaluate, to learn, to heal. Even if you have been in jail for many years and prison life is "life as usual" for you, the opportunity for growth and change is always there. In this seemingly most unlikely place of incarceration, a place where degradation and fear are ordinary, there is a unique opportunity to be lifted up, to be empowered, and to find peace.

Victor I never had time to get to know me until I was locked away alone with myself. Grace brought me to prison to be free of the self imposed prison I had myself locked away in all those years.

Still, not everyone is ready for inner healing. No one can make another person ready. Have you ever given advice to someone and they just weren't ready to hear it? Or have you ever been offered good advice you now wished you had listened to? Readiness comes in it's own time, if at all. Perhaps you've heard the expression, "you can lead a horse to water but you can't make it drink." A horse will only drink when it's thirsty. If there is some small thirst, some openness to change and growth, as I assume there is since you picked up this book, your environment need not stop you.

It is said that "life is like a stonemill. It will either polish you up or grind you down." Which your life will do is ultimately up to you. When you use your time as an opportunity to grow emotionally and spiritually, you are polished up. You are strengthened. You can increasingly feel good about who you are, what you have to offer, and the direction of your life — even if you are in prison — even if you're never going to get out.

Joe   I know being in jail or prison seems like the end of the road to most of us. But that's just not true. It can be the beginning of a new start.

CHAPTER 2

Who Are You, Anyway?

I WAS RECENTLY sitting in prison with a small group of men whom I had been meeting with for almost two years. Earlier that week I had sent them the first draft of this chapter. After reading it, a few of them had passed it on to other men who were interested in reading it as well. As we were sitting in the group that morning a young man whom I hadn't seen before came to the door. He asked if he could join us. He said that he had just read this chapter and that it had given him some answers he had been searching for. He said that for the past two years he had been repeatedly asking himself, "Who am I?," but that he couldn't find an answer that felt right. In frustration, he even went to friends, and asked them if they knew who he was.

This young man was way ahead of most us. He was searching for the answer to one of the most important questions one can ask — a question that most of us never stop to ask ourselves: "Who am I, really?" That's pretty amazing when you consider that who we believe we are effects every aspect of our life — how we feel about ourselves, how we treat others, who we gravitate toward as friends, how we use our time, what kind of goals we reach for, and what kind of choices we make. Too often we think we know who we are, when all we're doing is defining ourselves by a list of outer qualities, or by old tapes and messages given to us by hurt people and negative circumstances.

One of the best ways to use your time well and one of the most important things you can ever do, is get to know who you really are. By gaining a deeper understanding into yourself you will naturally find yourself feeling freer, better about yourself, less controlled by your circumstances, and more in control of your life. The first step in discovering who you are is to take stock of who you think you are now and what you believe about yourself. Many of us live with limited beliefs about who we are and who we can become, and it is essential to examine these beliefs or ideas about self in order to move beyond them.

PAUSE AND REFLECT

If someone asked you who you are, how would you respond?
Finish the following sentences:

I am _____.
I am _____.
I am _____.
I am _____.
I am _____.
I am _____.

After completing the sentences, reflect on your responses.
What do your responses tell you about yourself?
How do you see yourself?
What is most important to you?

Most people identify themselves by:
● the roles or acts they play — a mother, father, son, daughter, student, prisoner, ex-con, addict, gang member, enemy, friend, good person, cool person, carpenter, laborer, salesperson, etc.
● cultural heritage, sex and race — a man, woman, Italian, Irish, Asian, Hispanic, Afro-American.

- an emotional state and personality trait — insecure, secure, a perfectionist, hopeless, hard-working, lazy, angry, caring.

These labels describe certain aspects of our humanness and certain roles or ways of relating to the world that are familiar and habitual. But are these labels or roles the whole picture? Can they tell the whole truth about who you are? Have you ever noticed something even deeper and stronger than these roles within yourself? Maybe it happened when you fell in love. Or when your child was born. Or in connection with worship. Or just watching the sunrise one morning.

Most people have some experience of this other Self, even if it only happened once, and long ago at that. When I refer to the core Self, I use a capitol "S". Other terms to describe this Self are "free Self, greater Self, true Self, or essential Self." Exploring and coming to know this greater Self is at the heart of emotional healing and change. In order to start this exploration, I want to share a model of how we become who we are, one that goes beyond the emotions we identify with, the masks we wear, and the roles we play.

Most of us struggle to "be ourselves." But rarely do we understand what that really means. As infants we were all born into this world with unique personalities, unique qualities and traits that made Mike, Mike; Carol, Carol; me, me; and you, you. Each of us also was born with a free Self — a core of awareness and creative will whose job it is to help us fulfill our true nature, to become truly confident, loving, caring, and wise.

An ideal world would have provided us a safe, protective, and supportive environment to encourage our growth and positive potential. But clearly we don't live in an ideal world. More and more children of all races grow up with the harsh realities of poverty which leaves its scars on a child's sense of dignity. People of color are so often treated like second-class citizens in our society. Opportunities in employment, housing, education, and politics are often limited for minorities. Racism, classism, and poverty all play a part in reducing people's positive expectations for the future, as well as their feelings of self-worth.

All of this may have even been manageable if one had parents who were mature, loving, and supportive enough to counter-act some of the negative societal influences, and reliably reward and encourage a child's successes. But unfortunately, few of us had parents who could be counted on in this way. In order for a child to survive in an unsupportive world, he or she has to hide away their free and true Self and develop false selves instead — artificial creations of the mind — roles and ways of operating in the world that allow them to function and to survive — but at a great cost to their natural joy, wisdom, and health.

Perhaps your early years were loving and supportive and life started out okay. Perhaps you had a sense of safety and remember feeling loved and free — but then later something painful or awful happened: Dad left. Mom died. Your family was evicted from your home and you had no safe place to go. A drunk uncle crawled into your bed and molested you. Someone important to you was killed. Or perhaps your circle of friends changed and you went in a direction that led you toward trouble. Whatever happened, the world as you knew it before changed and you quickly closed down and had to erect a false self to endure it.

Before we ever left childhood, most of us forgot about our free Self completely. Instead of knowing that we were only acting out certain roles and attitudes in order to survive, we probably thought that we were those roles. We were that macho man; we were that cool dude, that tough girl, that person who had to take care of everybody, or that worthless nobody. Yet your core Self has never been absent and cannot be taken away — regardless of what you have done or what has been done to you. But it can be totally forgotten.

Small Selves, or Sub-Personalities

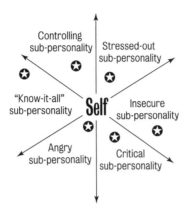

The above diagram shows the Self at the center of your being, and a variety of smaller selves around it. The small separated selves are also referred to as sub-personalities.* Although we may think of ourselves as one personality, in truth we each have many "sub-personalities," separate aspects of our being, each with distinct goals and characteristics that developed in order to cope with the life circumstance we found ourself in.

To the degree that we identify with any particular sub-personality, we see the world through the colored glasses (the beliefs and perspectives) of that particular identification.

Part of the process of growing up, of healthy personality development, includes developing and identifying with many sub-personalities — with the *emotions* we feel, the *acts or roles* we adopt, and the *beliefs* we hold. Many sub-personalities are an essential part of a whole and healthy human being. Yet *over–identifying with any one of them can debilitate us or stunt our growth.*

---

*The words sub-personality, small self, false self, conditioned self, limited self, and ego can all be used interchangeably.

The sub-personalities we could identify with are endless. Some examples are the angry sub-personality, the frustrated sub-personality, or the bitter, happy, or hopeless sub-personality. One could be identified with an act or role like The Bully, The Perfectionist, The Rescuer, Good Girl, Mean Mother, The Victim, The Kid, Druggie, Sex King or Queen, The Controller, The Judge. Or one could be identified with a belief like the "I'm never going to make it" sub-personality, or the "I know it all already" sub-personality, the "I'm a failure" or "Nothing is ever going to change" sub-personality.

Some of these may be both facts as well as acts. For example, you may indeed be a victim. That may be a fact. However, you may also identify with being a victim in such a way that it becomes "The Victim" act. Then it may become an excuse for justifying certain feelings while not making the effort to change and move on as best you can.

Or, you may indeed have been a failure as a parent if you were never there for your children. That may be a fact. But getting lost in the belief that "I am a failure as a parent" can be used as an excuse for not taking responsibility now. Even if your children are thirty and forty years old, you can reach out and do all you can to try to establish a bond of friendship now.

Or, you may have many reasons to be angry and you may feel angry much of the time. This may be a fact. But getting lost in the emotion of anger all the time — in the angry sub-personality — prevents you from being open to other feelings. In other words, you lock yourself in, becoming a prisoner of your own anger. Being aware of how this works opens you to the possibility of being released.

All of us develop sub-personalities in childhood that we bring along with us into adulthood. The more unsafe or traumatic our childhood, the more we will identify with fear-based feelings of anger, rage, insecurity, shame, guilt, despair, powerlessness. Rather than taking the natural course of all human emotions that arise and pass away from time to time, they become an established part of our thinking and feeling. We walk around relating to people and circumstances from the distorted and limited perspective of "the insecure sub-personality" or "the angry sub-personality." For instance, whenever we feel disappointed or hurt, we yell and blame those around us.

Every child needs to feel loved, respected, and safe. When children don't get these needs met they find ways of feeling and acting to protect themselves, to help them to feel safe. Imagine a three-year old who can only get his need for attention met when he is manipulative, when he cries, is loud, and acts "bad." He is likely to (unconsciously) decide that manipulating people is the best way to get what he needs or wants. "The Manipulator" sub-personality is being formed.

This is a creative and reasonable reaction for a three year old. It may still be creative at age five or ten. But if this person is now twenty or thirty, forty or fifty and is still manipulating people by acting loud, demanding, seductive, or aggressive as a way to get what he wants, it is obviously no longer creative. Now it is an old, outdated way of relating that is sure to inhibit, among other things, happiness, real friendship, and love.

Although the role of manipulator was first adopted to secure attention and love from others, now it is most likely to be met with fear, judgment, annoyance, and anger from others. Like many of the roles that become a way of life, the role of manipulator has outlived its usefulness, preventing the person lost in this role from finding other, more positive and mature ways of relating. Rather than being a mask that he's temporarily wearing, one that can be taken off at will, the act becomes like a permanent fixture to the personality.

Once we're stuck in a sub-personality or false self, most of us flesh out the role with experiences, attitudes, beliefs and behaviors that fit it — and then we reinforce this false self again and again. If we think of ourselves as the "Know It All" then we're likely to be close-minded and think no one has anything valuable to teach us. If we identify with the "I can't do it" sub-personality, we will immediately feel anxious and helpless when a new situation presents itself to us. The more anxious we feel, the less able we are to think through the necessary steps. And the more frustrated we become the more likely we are to feel defeated. We prove to ourselves what we believed all along — we "can't do it."

We also call this false self a conditioned or limited self because it only sees, feels, thinks and acts in ways that are familiar and programmed. Sadly the false selves live life in an unconscious state, acting much like mechanical robots.

As you begin to become aware of certain sub-personalities, it's important not to judge yourself. Believe it or not, all of these were formed in reaction to not feeling good enough, loved, safe, or respected (most of them when you were a child). Or they formed in reaction to certain patterns in the family. We often take on the same attitudes, behaviors, and roles that are modeled by the people we grow up around. They all had very reasonable reasons for forming. As you become aware of them the most important thing to remember is that they are *not* you. Don't confuse them with who You really are.

If we become chronically identified with our sub-personalities, like actors who get lost in the parts they are playing, we forget that we are the director of the play as well as the actors.

Hank My acts are pretty much my life. I've often said to a friend "I want to be an actor." The reason for this was because I always knew deep down that I wasn't the person I was projecting myself to be. Roles that I have played were drug dealer instead of drug addict, rich man instead of poor man, someone who shuns love instead of someone who was afraid of it, someone who cares when I didn't. Upon entering adulthood (I'm twenty-two) I've found myself not knowing who I really am. It really is time that I discovered who I am and who I want to be.

In order to grow into our full human potential we need to become aware of the roles, emotions and beliefs with which we identify. We need to go beyond identifying with just our partial selves to an awareness of our core Self so that we can have our emotions, roles and beliefs without being limited by them. Getting lost in a sub-personality in a chronic way is the same as being confined to an inner prison. There are no life sentences in this prison unless we stay unaware of what is operating in our own minds and hearts. The Self always has the key and we are our own jailer.

Stepping Back

PAUSE AND REFLECT

Imagine it is 4:45 in the afternoon and you promised someone that you would make an important phone call to them at 4:30. Count usually ends by 4 P.M. but something is going on and count still hasn't ended. You are getting more anxious and impatient, your body is getting tenser by the moment, you're getting angrier and you know that not only will you be late but you'll now have to compete with other inmates to get to the phone first. In your mind your anger is turning on the person you have to call. And you're thinking about the worst possible consequences of not making the call when you said you would....

Now imagine a moment in the middle of freaking out when you clearly get that your impatience and anger isn't getting you to the phone any sooner. Imagine that you then take some deep breaths and tell yourself to relax. You think about the situation and realize there's nothing you can do to change the circumstance. You decide to relax, knowing you'll make the call as soon as you can. You think about how you will just explain what happened to the person you're going to call. You put on your radio and feel more relief. You remind yourself that you do have a choice as to how you respond to this

situation, and you tell yourself that you might as well relax. You lie
back, breathe deeply, and enjoy the music on your favorite station.

In this scenario you make the shift from being lost in the small selves — in this case the "impatient self", "anxious self", "angry self" — to being identified with the core, essential, or greater Self — the part of you that *is aware* of different ways of relating to the situation *and chooses the wisest and most productive option available.*

Self-awareness develops when we keep growing and maturing into emotionally healthy adults. With self-awareness we have the ability to stand back and observe which sub-personalities are operating. Instead of being lost in frustration or anger while you're waiting to make your phone call, with self-awareness you're able to watch yourself getting caught up in the frustration and anger. And you're able to make the choice to relate to the situation differently. This kind of awareness allows you to recognize that there is more to you than the emotion, role, or belief that you are experiencing at any particular moment. Recognizing this is the first step in shifting from experiencing the world through the eyes of the small self or sub-personality to the more expansive perspective of the greater Self.

The ability *to step back and be aware* of yourself getting caught up in impatience and anxiety and the ability *to choose* to respond in a clear, wise, and deliberate way are natural functions of the Self.

The Self: Lost and Found

People who are not anchored within their Self don't realize their intrinsic value and self-worth as human beings and, as a result, aren't likely to value others. They lack self-esteem. Sadly, few of us enter adulthood having learned to feel good about ourselves.

When we are limited by certain chronic sub-personalities, not only are we inhibited from being objectively aware and free to respond to the situations at hand, but we are also blocked from the many other innate qualities of the Self. When we are aligned with our Self we naturally experience greater wisdom, trust in ourselves, inner strength and peace, courage, optimism, creativity, humor, responsibility, compassion, and love. We discover greater effectiveness, and access the confidence and power to act on our deepest instincts of what is right.

When we are aligned with our Self we are aware of a fundamental goodness within — a goodness that is undiluted. Every person has this fundamental goodness, but many are starkly disconnected from it. Did you ever meet a baby or young child given reliable love and emotional safety, whose nature was not good? Unless there is a chemical imbalance and mental illness or severe abuse and deprivation that thwart healthy expression, every child radiates this fundamental goodness. As children, if that goodness is not reflected back to us by parents, teachers, and other adults, somewhere along the way we begin to lose contact with it and become disconnected. As we align with the Self and heal, we re-connect with that goodness. And that connection brings with it strength and peace.

Being aligned with our true Self quite consistently is an experience that few of us in "civilized" society have had. Very few people, especially in our culture, have been consciously aware of the existence of the Self. And yet the Self is always where we are.

Throughout this book you will learn ways to connect and align with the core Self while developing understanding and patience for those aspects of the personality which, out of their conditioning, fear, and feelings of unworthiness, have taken center stage and undermined your genuine power and freedom in the past.

But first, let's take a look at emotional healing and how it connects to this concept of Self and sub-personality.

What Is Emotional Healing?

To be healed is to be whole. But what does it mean to be whole? Victor's experience gives us a powerful sense of what it can mean: "When I take an honest look into myself I see all the hurt, the denial, dishonesty, manipulation, numbing, fear, and all the feelings of inadequacy. I also see a love, an unconditional love, an awareness of my true Self, of gentleness, kindness, and patience. These new feelings are bringing light to the darker side of me, exposing them so that I will find the door to my heart."

To be whole is to open to all of who we are, our dark side as well as our light; our small selves as well as our greater Self. Opening to all of who we are takes the willingness to look honestly at ourselves. It also requires a certain amount of skillful guidance. Often we don't see that there is more to us than our small selves because we don't know how to look. Sometimes people are convinced that they know everything about themselves already. One inmate commented, "I never gave certain feelings a chance to reveal themselves and as a consequence never even knew myself, and all the time I thought I knew everything." Sometimes we don't look inward because we're sure that we won't like what we find. We may think all we'll find is negative traits or feelings of guilt, sadness, regret, etc. It is our greatest fear that this is it. This is the whole picture. The show stops here. But healing is the process of restoring our awareness to the reality that has always existed but from which we have been alienated — that we have a basic nature of goodness and power. Healing is re-membering what is ours to begin with.

It takes courage to heal because it requires that we acknowledge and accept what we may have rejected in ourselves. For Victor, it took looking directly at things about himself that drug and alcohol abuse had allowed him to ignore and deny for years: the dishonesty, manipulation, numbing, fear, and feelings of inadequacy. Choosing to heal meant he would have to honestly look at his mistakes, but without beating himself up for making them. It meant looking at aspects of his personality that he didn't like, aspects of himself that had threatened a self-image of himself as a good guy. He had to look at parts of himself that he had locked away inside himself. It meant he would have to be willing to start looking at the underlying fear, pain, and feelings of worthlessness that propelled his addiction and criminal behavior.

Healing also meant that he would discover the goodness and beauty, — yes, beauty — of his true nature. Opening to this reality is sometimes the hardest part of healing for men and women in prison. Society's messages, personal history, and a deep-seated insecurity from years of deceptive messages, all conspire to hide this possibility from awareness.

As Victor also wrote, "Opening my heart to both good and bad has made me a new creation and given me understanding of the self worth of both myself and my fellow man." As we heal, we realize that there is a great deal more to life than what meets the (small) self's eyes.

Until we consciously heal, the connection with our true nature, with our spiritual core, is severed. Healing is making this connection. If you look only to the outside world to restore this connection, to restore your worth, to affirm your fundamental goodness, you are looking in the wrong place. Beneath the outer world of illusion your worthiness and your goodness are facts.

PART 2

CHAPTER 3

The Long and Winding Road: From Childhood to Prison

IN ORDER TO know your true Self you need to go back and look at how you became the person you are today. It's hard and often painful to look back at your childhood. But the choices you made in reaction to your childhood shape your personality and effect your life in countless ways.

Ron I grew up with six sisters and two brothers in a city project that was a dog eat dog world. My father was out working all the time and when he was home he was always drunk and fighting with my mother. My mother was secretive and cold. She disciplined me with slaps, a yard stick hit across my back and legs, and if I really misbehaved, I was hit with a coat hanger and a broom stick. I always felt unsafe and on guard and never got love, affection or support. I felt like I was one big mistake, like I was no good and never would be.

Age 12: Father removed from home by police.

Age 13: Molested by an adult friend.

Age 15: Committed to DYS (Department of Youth Services).

Age 17: Girlfriend became pregnant. I took off to Florida.

Age 14 to 35: Alcoholism and drug addiction; worsened as time went by.

Age 14 to 28: Hustled the street for money. Men would pay me for sex.

Age 19: Joined U.S.Army. Went to Vietnam.

Age 20: Came back from Vietnam.

Age 23: Arrested for assault and battery with a dangerous weapon.

Age 33: Arrested for assault and battery with a dangerous weapon.

Age 37: Arrested for murder. Sentenced to life imprisonment.

Juan Born in Puerto Rico. My mother drank at the time she was pregnant with me and was beat constantly by my father.

Under age 5: Ever since I can remember I have been beaten.

Age 6: I had to work at home and in the sugar cane fields from age six on. If I ever got caught playing, I would be beaten.

Age 8: I stole five dollars from my grandmother and got beaten for about five straight days by my mother.

Age 9: My father was drunk and beating my mother, after he finished with her he beat me and grabbed me by the arm and threw me in the air like an airplane. I landed on my face. To this day, I still have scars on my body. He beat me with a belt buckle as I got older.

Age 12: I was sexually abused by my uncle.

Age 14: I quit school and began to work with other farmers in flower gardens to make money to help my family.

Age 15: My mother died.

Age 15-18: Continued working with other farmers and after work cooked for my father and my younger siblings.

Age 18: Came to N.Y. Lived with my oldest brother and worked.

Age 19: My first experience with marijuana. Got involved with street gang and drank heavily.

Age 21: Had a common-law wife. I treated her the same way I learned from my father. Thanks God, after three years I stopped beating her.

Age 23-28: Used heroin.

Age 24: My first and second encounter with the law. First one for breaking and entering a meat store at night. For that charge I served fifty days in a county jail. Second, I got busted with five two dollar bags of cocaine. For this charge I did not show up in court. I stopped working and sold heroin to support my habit.

Age 25-26: Used cocaine and had one arrest for disturbing the peace. I also committed myself in a hospital to try to quit my addiction, but they were getting me hooked on methadone and what I needed the most was counseling, so I left the hospital.

Age 26: Arrested for murder and possession of heroin. Given a first degree life sentence.

Stan My parents were divorced by the time I was three and the only memories of my father were of drunkenness and fighting with my mom. I felt that there wasn't much hope at a happy life and that was the way all families were and that was the way they were supposed to be. I thought all families went through the hell I was subjected to on a daily basis — that all fathers (and stepfathers) beat their wives and children. Basically I thought that family life was waiting for your dad to come home from the bar and hoping that he wasn't in a bad mood. I really thought that was the way every one lived, but that wasn't living, it was dying a degree at a time without knowing it.

Vic There was only one fight or argument that my parents had that I saw, and even this I can't remember well. My parents never drank or used drugs and seemed to be happy but I never witnessed any affection between them. They slept in different rooms. I was never shown any affection either. There were never any hugs or kisses. My uncle who lived downstairs drank heavily and was abusive to his children and me. I could never do anything right around him.

When I thought about my school experiences the first teacher to come to mind was Sister Margaret. She had bumps all over her face. Large bumps. She used to seem to pick on me. I remember her bringing me to the front of the class many times and beating me over the hand with a leg of a chair. She also held me back saying that Catholic Schools were way ahead of public school. So for two years I watched my friends move ahead while I seemed to be going backwards.

Ralph By the time I was ten years old, I fully believed I was bad and unlovable. But worse than that was I hated myself for making my mother "have to put me away." While in reform school I was beaten and raped. I thought I deserved all of it and never questioned it being right or wrong.

Abuse and neglect are a common thread running through the childhood of most prisoners. If I wrote a brief description of the stories of childhood abuse from the women and men who participated in the Emotional Awareness/Emotional Healing classes, this book would easily be double its size. Most prisoners didn't live with both parents while growing up. According to the Bureau of Justice Statistics more than twenty-five percent have parents who abused drugs or alcohol. Many of the men I have met who committed murder had been sexually molested as children. Many had lived in foster homes and spent years under youth correctional departments. Many people who end up in prison grow up poor. Most had no role model of an emotionally healthy, responsible adult in their family.

You may be among the minority of prisoners who feel that your childhood did not play a role in setting the stage for prison. A few of the participants in the Emotional Awareness course felt this way. Some people seemed to have a specific incident or a particular life crisis as a teenager or young adult that preceded getting into trouble — like the death of a family member or fighting in Vietnam.

Despite apparently safe and loving childhoods, some experienced school and adolescence as difficult and meaningless. They weren't willing to listen to their parent's advice and instead started hanging with "the wrong crowd." For many who grew up in poor, unsafe neighborhoods, gangs were the only crowds around. Even if you don't feel your childhood had much or anything to do with you being in prison, I encourage you to read on and stay open to what's written here. I repeatedly meet people who don't think that this work is relevant to their life at first, and as they look closer things come to mind that surprise them and offer fresh and important insight.

I have frequently met women and men in prison who had been seriously abused as children but they (1) had no idea that they had been abused, and (2) had no idea how their childhood had influenced their choices and affected the way their lives turned out. Juan is a good example of this. Look back at Juan's life (on the second page of this chapter), and you will see that he was totally robbed of his childhood and beaten severely on a regular basis. A few years before I met him, Juan wrote a paper in which he described himself as coming from a good, decent family. He honestly thought of his childhood as a happy one. Many men and women grow up in cultures where beating and abusing children is commonplace. If that is all you know and see, then you naturally think it is reasonable, just, and fair behavior. Childhood abuse is never any of these. And child abuse is *never* a child's fault. As you will read, the fall-out from being treated disrespectfully, neglectfully, and abusively is enormous. It may be a good part of the reason you are where you are today.

Recognizing the negative influences in one's life does not in any way excuse a person from being accountable for their behavior. What it does is open the door to the inner healing and creative power that is needed to have a future different from the past. In truth, there are few, if any, adults that do not have some wounds from their childhood to heal.

PAUSE AND REFLECT

Think back on the lives of the people on the first few pages of this chapter. Was your life like any of these? When you were a child did you feel uncomfortable or unsafe around certain people?

Were you emotionally, physically, or sexually abused as a child?

Were there adults you could count on to give you love, respect, and support as a child and teenager?

Did you have a parent or other caretaker who you could count on to protect you if needed while growing up?

Did you feel emotionally and physically safe?

Was there someone you could rely on for mature guidance?

In the last chapter, I explained how we all start life as basically good, in touch with our free Self. Every one of us also starts our life out as a totally vulnerable, dependent child. When our needs for reliable safety and love aren't met in order to survive emotionally, we send our bright, trusting and delightful child spirit underground and lock it away for self-protection. In her book, *Recovery of Your Inner Child*, author Lucia Capacchione writes, "but the Inner Child never grows up and never goes away. It remains buried alive, waiting to be set free. And we can't build a truly workable, happy adult world on the shaky foundations of a frightened and isolated child who never got it's basic needs met."

When the adults in our life can't be counted on for love and respect, we keep growing physically but a part of our emotional growth and development gets slowed down or even totally held back. Our willingness to trust people, to be open, spontaneous, and loving goes underground. We build walls around our inner child to try to make sure that she or he doesn't get hurt again. Walls of toughness, walls of emotional deadness, walls of anger and defiance, all to protect that sweet and vulnerable child who waits there scared, hurting, and angry.

When our basic needs for *reliable* love, comforting, and safety aren't met, it brings about a state of chronic anxiety, fear, shame, anger, emotional isolation, and despair in our inner child that follows us into adulthood. All addiction and most recurring emotional and physical problems in adulthood are a sign that the wounded child within us is trying to get our attention. He or she is still scared and waiting for the missing sense of love and safety. If we want to heal, we can't neglect this part of ourselves. For us to be healthy adults, as strange as it may seem at first, we must pay attention to the child within, embrace him or her, and learn to re-parent and be there for ourselves with the compassion and patience that was missing before.

When I present the idea of working with the wounded inner child in prison classes, some people are skeptical at first. For one thing, as you certainly know, prison is often the last place that people feel safe to open up. There is the survival instinct to put up even more walls around oneself in prison. And there's the additional inclination to make sure these walls are well barricaded.

I often meet inmates who lived on the edge on the outside — trafficking drugs and/or seriously abusing people — who become frightened at the prospect of doing this work, of meeting up with the feelings inside themselves that their addiction had kept them away from. Some feel looking back into the past will open up a can of worms they don't want to see. Or they initially feel this isn't the time or place. I understand and respect the reluctance and the resistance to doing this work. Sometimes the resistance is a healthy sign that it isn't the time and place to bring your inner child out of hiding (even if it is in the privacy of your own mind or with a counselor, someone from the ministry, or a group you feel you can trust). But I find that most people who are interested in attending the classes I teach (or people who pick this book up and have the interest to read it) *can* do this work and find enormous benefit from it.

I consistently notice a few things that may support your being open to the inner child work. One is that people have a way of un-consciously knowing and not bringing to awareness more than they are ready to deal with at the time. Another is that the benefits you get from meeting and spending time with your inner child far ex-ceed the risk you take. Unfortunately, when a person has been wounded in childhood and hasn't had the awareness, support, and guidance to heal some of the wounds, the child who is still "buried alive" always contaminates life in the present. Most inmates who I have supported in this work find that "inner child work" shines a light on a missing link to self-understanding and allows them to make sense of their life and emotionally heal in a way that has not been possible before.

If you don't feel ready, willing, or safe enough to really get into the exercises later in this chapter, just reading the chapter can be very helpful and increase your self-understanding. If your childhood was really abusive, going back and acknowledging what was too painful to feel before is difficult and courageous work.

Jose My understanding of myself is now very different from when I began this class. The inner child work has changed me in ways I never thought possible. I have found that my life was a result of many factors that were hidden until this work began. Now I have come to a much better place in understanding why I am what I am and how to be the way that I can be.

Andy Being able to get in touch with my "Inner Child" has opened doors within me which I thought was closed and shut forever. I was able to face some of my past with new courage and dignity.

Why Bother Going Back?

The following letter was written by my friend Katie to her brother Ben while he was in a drug rehabilitation center for cocaine addiction. It, and Ben's response are examples of the insight and healing that people who go back into their childhoods can bring to their present lives.

Dear Ben,

This letter is about me, but I'm writing it for you...

I am a 41 year old woman who has a very little girl inside who hurts a lot. She's hidden away, often not consciously present even to myself, but has been forever hurting, hurting and hurting.

The hurt started when this little girl was a real little girl. She craved love, she craved to be held, and she craved to be special. But this little girl grew up with a mother who also had a very hurt little girl inside, a mother who couldn't show love, especially in any physical way, like hugging her child, because the hurt little girl inside her had probably never been held herself. Thus, the little girl inside me learned to believe she was unlovable.

As a child, the little girl longed to be accepted, valued, and appreciated. But this little girl grew up with a father who had a hurt little boy inside himself who believed he was stupid and not good enough. He tried to teach his little girl to be good enough by trying to create a "thinking mind" by challenging and debating everything that the child said. Instead, the little girl learned that whatever she said, thought or believed was wrong. The little girl learned she was stupid.

The real little girl wanted to do things "right", wanted to be "good enough", wanted to be the best she could be but because her parents had children inside them who believed they weren't good enough, everything their child did was also not good enough. They were very critical of their child, stressing the shortfalls in accomplishments and the neglect (stupidity!) in the failures. The child learned she could never be good enough.

The real little girl would get angry because she was hurt and couldn't get her needs met. But, anger was very destructive and painful in her house. Both parents had very angry children inside them and expressed that anger in unhealthy ways. Anger became very dangerous and hurtful, sometimes physically, but more so emotionally. Sarcastic comments, terrible fights, loud noises that smashed against the child's innermost feelings leaving behind an aftershock that has survived a lifetime. The child learned to become invisible. The child learned it was never safe to express her angry feelings. The child learned to be a sponge that soaks up anger and keeps it from spreading.

The real little girl "knew" instinctively that love was vital but had no way to feel love and no way to express love because love was lost in the hurt and pain of generations. This little girl learned she was trapped in hopelessness... a life without love.

This little girl learned to cope with the hurt by "stuffing" it deeper and deeper inside... and taking her very self with it. She kept very busy... Working too much, trying to do too much and never relaxing or daring to because then the pain would rise up and hurt too much to bare. But the pain turned to a constant ache and she learned to try to cope with it by planning her death- not to kill herself as much as to kill the pain. She tried to find ways to numb the ache... tranquilizers, anti-depressants and always knowing the ultimate relief would be alcohol. But, the little girl grew up with her alcoholic parents and feared alcoholism more then the pain so she forced herself (most of the time) not to drink. The little girl became exhausted.

Ben, as I said this letter is about me but it is for you. You grew up with the same hurting parents that I had and inside you there is a hurting little boy. Maybe that little boy "learned" different things than the little girl in this letter but I'm sure that the things that the little boy learned are not true. Ben, I want so much for you to feel the love that I have for you. I want to comfort you, to hold you and to help you carry your pain until it's not so heavy. The only way that I can think of to do that right now is to write you this letter in the hopes that sharing what I've come to realize might help you see that there are very real reasons why you hurt inside. It is understandable that you have been looking all your life for ways to cope and ease the pain. I hope that you will continue with therapy after your discharge. Maybe it would be helpful if you show this letter to your counselor as a way to begin (or continue) looking at what untruths the little boy inside you learned and as a start toward healing that little boy.

I have a very clear image of the little boy inside you (he's adorable by the way! big blue eyes with a wonderfully impish twinkle in them!) and I'm holding that little boy with all the love in my heart.

I love you Ben no matter where you are or what is happening in your life. I'll keep in touch and please call me anytime.

Love,
Katie

Ben's reply

Dear Katie,

Well, I've been debating with myself whether to write or to call. This debate has been raging for a week. This is my last day here [drug rehab. center] and I've decided to write.

I have not been able to read your letter a second time, but I will when I get the nerve. This letter is taking about 15 minutes per sentence- I can't seem to find the words.

Prior to coming here the ideas in your letter would have meant nothing. However, as a result of being just slightly more receptive, I was allowed to have the most profound revelation as to who and why I am. For the first time in my life I felt that I might understand me, and I knew that at least someone else did. One reason why I need to read the letter again is because I cried through most of it — in fact I was still crying 45 minutes later while running around the track. When I cried it was like a tremendous release of pressure.

I've been looking back at all the major decisions of my life and now have some insight as to why I always went the wrong way. Even the decisions that appear to have been right were made for the wrong reasons.

I could write on and on — but for now Katie, know that I love you
very much and I can't put into words what your letter meant to me.
Love,
Ben

If we don't do the work of healing our wounded inner child, our
life becomes contaminated by the oozing wounds that remain below the surface. In the last ten years, John Bradshaw, author, therapist, and popular workshop leader, has made the importance of "inner child work" well known. (His lectures on the inner child have
been shown on public television stations throughout the U.S.) In his
book *Homecoming: Reclaiming and Championing Your Inner Child*,
Bradshaw writes about how when the inner child is left alone, un-
recognized, unloved, and therefore, unhealed, he or she inevitably
contaminates one's adult life. As you read this and the following
chapter, reflect on your own life and how this is true for you.

Until we slow down, look inward, and really give our patient attention to the wounded child within, there is an unconscious *com-
pulsion* to keep repeating the same behaviors that have made life un-
manageable in the past. A leading figure in the field of psychology,
Carl Jung once wrote, "the psychological rule says that when an inner situation is not made conscious, it happens outside as fate." If
there is pain inside and it is not made conscious (in other words, if
we are unaware of the pain, or too scared or numb to honestly acknowledge it and meet it with compassion), then we find ourselves
stuck in a life filled with pain. And we will probably find ourselves
creating a great deal of pain for others as well.

A woman whose father beat her or her mother and who hasn't
dealt with the pain from her past, may find herself in one relationship after another with men who are abusive. In such a situation, the
abusive men are ultimately responsible for their choice to use violence. But as an adult, the woman has the opportunity to learn that
she has alternatives to a life of abuse and to move beyond the old

and familiar. (Part of her healing requires recognizing that *no matter what she did, nothing justifies physical abuse.*)

A man whose mother never showed up for him emotionally may find himself married to a woman who is not really there for him emotionally. A person who hated that a parent was an addict finds himself or herself an addict as well. Until the inner child's pain is honored — like it or not — we keep replaying the same old story.

We begin to heal and our life takes on new meaning and possibility when we visit the inner child in his or her solitary confinement and help release them from the prison of their pain. The woman who grew up around the abusive father needs to listen with compassion and patience to the sweet young girl within her who was left terrified and hurting. The man needs to listen with compassion and patience to the pain, fear and deep sadness of the wonderful little boy inside him who, like all children, needed a compassionate and patient mother. They both need to listen and comfort the child within who was left emotionally abandoned, rejected, and shamed for needing the love and safety that was only perfectly natural to need.

Acknowledging the neglect, disrespect, and abuse from the vantage point of both the inner child and adult Self, leads to emotional healing. You do the work of going back to your childhood suffering in order to finish the past and move on with greater self-respect, freedom, and creative power.

Childhood Shame

One of the most damaging legacies of a neglected and abused childhood is what Bradshaw calls "toxic shame." Unlike guilt that comes from something that you do (for example, you feel guilty because you are caught stealing, cheating, lying, etc.), toxic shame comes from a feeling that you are bad, inadequate, or a problem just because you exist. It develops in childhood when rather than feeling welcome in your world, you feel like a burden. Toxic shame develops when your natural and basic need for love, security, caring attention, and safety seem like too much to ask for or expect. You are shamed for wanting and needing what is natural.

If we grow up in a situation where we don't feel loved and re-spected for being ourselves, with the limited reasoning of a child we come to believe things like we're not a good person, we're really not worth loving, we're something less than a beautiful, wonderful cre-ation. Toxic shame is not about what we did, it is about who we are. It creates deep-seated confusion and a serious distortion in one's self-concept; we feel ashamed just for being who we are. Rather than see that "this situation is not good" a child comes to believe, "I am no good." Because a child isn't capable of understanding that "the people I count on aren't capable of loving at this time," the child comes to believe, "I am not lovable." When a child is disci-plined without love, rather than understanding that "I made a mis-take," a child comes to believe, "I *am* a mistake." Unless the belief is examined and rejected, it follows us throughout our life.

All children who are victims of abuse, (whether emotional, phys-ical, sexual) blame themselves in some way. They *falsely* believe that the abuse was their fault or at the very least, they should somehow be able to help fix it. When a child is abused, it is *never* their fault. If you were abused as a child, it was *not* your fault.

....

PAUSE AND REFLECT

Stop for a few moments and take a few relaxing breaths. Then think back into your childhood. Return in your mind to the home(s) and neighborhood(s) where you grew up. As you think back, do you recall an incident or pattern of neglect, abuse, or disrespect from an adult that you blame yourself for? If so, take a while to imagine the child within you who felt ashamed or guilty for what happened. Imagine opening your heart to that child and letting them know in no uncertain terms, *that it was not their fault. Then re-assure him or her that it was not their fault again and again and again.*

It is time to give up the illusion and lie that childhood neglect and abuse — *even if* you misbehaved, *even if* you participated in certain acts without obvious resistance (i.e. childhood sexual abuse) — was your fault. Let the shame and guilt you experienced as a child come up and be met and witnessed with the compassion and wisdom of your greater Self. If you have kept shameful childhood secrets hidden, try to share them with someone who is compassionate and trustworthy. Telling them to someone safe helps you to heal the wounds and recover from the shame. Recovery happens when you can name the truth and receive the validation, compassion, and understanding that is needed. Keeping secrets deadens a part of us and stops the healing of our emotions and spirit. Telling the truth brings the heart back to life. Until you address these issues in some way, you (and your inner child) live with self-blame and with it, a degree of self-torture. The secrets that you keep locked away keep you shame-ful and stop you from appreciating and resting in your intrinsic innocence and goodness.

In addition to the personal experiences of shame within our families, many individuals experience a cultural shame that reinforces toxic shame. We live in a profoundly shaming culture where people are shamed for being poor, shamed for being a minority, shamed for having learning problems, shamed for being a victim, shamed for making mistakes, shamed for "not being successful." By virtue of circumstance, many people come to see themselves as personal failures. Being incarcerated can produce another layer of significant shame. Unless you have loving support from others or a rich spiritual life to draw from, it can be very difficult to feel good about yourself and lift yourself above this chronic, painful state of shame. Fortunately, many psychologists and spiritual teachers have looked

long and hard at this problem and have mapped out clear trails leading to recovery and healing. The chapters that follow will provide
you with guidance for this journey.

CHAPTER 4

The Fallout From Childhood Wounding ...and How to Start Recovery

Now THAT WE know that there is a little kid in each of us who often didn't get what he or she needed, it's time to begin to meet those needs. It's never too late. First, though, let's look more specifically at four ways your wounded inner child might effect your life and how she or he has played a significant role in your being where you are today.

How Keeping Your Inner Child Hostage Contaminates Your Life

OFFENDER BEHAVIORS

Bradshaw writes, "We tend to think that all people who have a wounded inner child are nice, quiet people. But, in fact, the wounded inner child is responsible for much of the violence and cruelty in the world." Severe emotional, physical, and sexual childhood abuse are the training ground for becoming an offender. At the root of most offender behavior is the unhealed anger, rage, grief, guilt, and shame from childhood violence. As you may know, a high percentage of sex offenders were sexually abused as children. Many batterers witnessed high levels of violence between their parents and were victims themselves.

To be a victim of childhood abuse makes a person feel weak and vulnerable. Although it is a totally distorted impulse, one of the ways a deeply wounded person counteracts the feeling of weakness is to become the victimizer. The abused becomes the abuser. *If you are in prison for victimizing others, part of your healing requires that you get in touch with your own victimization.* If, with as much of a spirit of non-judging acceptance toward yourself as you can summon, you begin to allow some of your pain to have a voice and tell it's story, you will be strengthened. With this strength you will be able to increasingly be there for the child in you who was victimized and who so desperately needs your love.

When possible, talk about your own abuse with someone you trust. Tell your story. Tell it to God. Tell it to your own highest Self. Tell it to a counselor. Write out what happened and how you felt from the perspective of your inner child — even if you rip it up and through it away moments later. When you give the child within an opportunity to safely feel some of the pain, fear, anger, and sadness that it was not safe for them to feel before, then the impulse or the need to take part in an offender or criminal behavior begins to recede and be healed.

ACTING OUT / ACTING IN BEHAVIORS

The wounded inner child may act out their pain by being insensitive, mean, and rebellious. Look around you and notice the people who are acting out a lot. Notice the people who get one disciplinary report after another. Notice the people who go around intimidating other inmates. Notice who acts loud and obnoxious. Notice who acts like the world revolves around what they want. Notice those who "act like children." Rather than judging these people, consider that it is the wounded inner child contaminating their life and relationships. When you see people like this, it's an excellent bet that it is the wounded child within them who is propelling their acting out. Often the meaner and more abusive a person is, the more abusive their childhood and the more wounded they are.

Although you may see a wounded inner child beneath these be-haviors, it doesn't mean that you don't do what you need to do to handle a situation. It is likely though, that seeing the drama from a more mature perspective may help you to maintain some emotional distance and not get so pulled in.

Sometimes the wounded child acts the pain in rather than out by hurting themselves physically or putting themself down with constant self-judgment. A child who is abused or put down always internal-izes the abusive parent, teacher, or society to one degree or another. As they get older, they don't need others to tell them they're a whore, a thug, stupid, bad, or good-for-nothing. They will uncon-sciously do it to themselves. The painful emotions of the inner child that don't get resolved and expressed in healthy ways get turned inward into negative self-talk, self-hatred and shame, and into feel-ings of emptiness and depression. When children grow up in environments that don't affirm their intrinsic goodness, they adopt a false self to survive and become disconnected from their own true nature.

When we create a safe place in our hearts and minds for our inner child to begin to feel safe and share the truth about their pain, we begin to heal the pain and move beyond the negative and limiting beliefs that were adopted without question.

ADDICTIVE/COMPULSIVE BEHAVIORS

The wounded inner child is at the core of perhaps all addictions and addictive behavior. Research indicates that there may be a genetic predisposition toward alcoholism and chemical dependency. Even if there are genetic factors, genetics is never the only reason one picks up the bottle (or whatever). Until the child within is given the love, attention, and care he or she has been craving for years, one can stop drinking, drugging, or whatever and the addiction (crav-ing) just gets transferred from one thing to another: Not drinking but compulsively watching T.V. for ten hours a day. Not drugging but working fourteen hours a day. Not using sex as the object of an addiction but gaining thirty pounds and gambling every chance there is. Not gambling anymore but attaching oneself to religion not as a genuine quest but as a distraction from the pain and emptiness inside. A need and a craving for loving attention in the inner child is most often at the core of addiction. For addiction to be healed, for abstinence and sobriety to mean freedom rather than a constant battle, our inner child needs to have this need met.

CO-DEPENDENCE

In an unhealthy family, all kinds of craziness goes on, but no one in the family is up front and calls a spade a spade. No one deals with the real issues. No one calls the alcoholic mother on her drinking and confronts her with how devastating her behavior is to her children. No one calls the abusive father on his behavior and stands up and protects the children from the fallout. You learn early on that there's no one you can rely on and that your needs and feelings aren't really important. You don't get enough of the good things we all need. And you get too many of the negative things — and then you go into life handicapped by the needs that weren't met. With the resulting low self-esteem and painful inner life, the child naturally grows into an adult who, being disconnected from him or herself, tries to find fulfillment on the outside. One's sense of identity and importance becomes external — dependent on people and things such as money, the right job, a Harley, a Cadillac or BMW, a relationship, a "great" body, membership in a particular social group or gang. Without these external things there may be little or no sense of identity or self-worth. An extreme of the co-dependent is the woman or man who attempts suicide because their mate leaves. Not having themSelf when their partner leaves, they feel they are literally left with nothing. And the emptiness feels unbearable.

The twelve-step programs talk about the co-dependent as a person who assists the alcoholic or drug addict in keeping from honestly facing their addiction. The co-dependent, rather than truly helping their partner to deal with their difficulties honestly, will lie for them, live in denial, and cover things up. This co-dependent "helping," although it may be mistakenly done in the name of love, is always done out of fear and dependency. The co-dependent would rather be in a destructive relationship than confront the fear of setting limits and dealing with the situation honestly. Co-dependents learned a long time ago that their own needs weren't important. Lacking self-respect, they might do anything to get others to like them, accept them, and not leave.

Another way that co-dependency shows up is when people feel so impoverished inside that they take and take and take, with no sense of genuine appreciation or generosity. They have little or no sense of a healthy inter-dependent relationship in which each person respects his or her own needs, knows when to say yes and when to say no, and both people have some sense of respecting and honoring the needs of the other person as well.

Reflect on your close relationships. Do you pay attention to your own needs and honor them? Do you always put aside what you would like for another person (and then rationalize why you did it)? Are you frequently trying to please others to get their approval? Do you stand up for what you know is right and set limits when needed? Do you truly consider the well-being of others when making decisions?

When we don't do the work of inner healing and re-parenting ourselves, we usually go looking for a partner who will do it for us. But it never works. Most often we attract a person who has a wounded child within them. Both adults are looking for the other person to be the perfect mother or father. What usually happens is that the needs of both clash and are left unfulfilled.

When you connect with the child within and with his or her real feelings, you begin to feel more connected to yourSelf and to others in a more satisfying way. Your inner child needs you. Be gentle with yourself and when you are ready, let him or her know they have a friend.

Meeting Your Inner Child

As an adult you may feel so wounded that it seems difficult, if not impossible, for you to offer your inner child the love, compassion, and safety that she or he needs. You may even find yourself feeling contempt for or fear of your inner child. If you find yourself in a situation like this, it can be helpful, even though it may seem strange at first, to call into your imagination a wise and compassionate older man or woman, or a spiritual presence (God, Jesus, Mary, an angel, Allah) or anyone who you imagine has all the qualities that your inner child needs at this time. If you are open to this, you may find that the image of a wise and spiritual presence has the potential to evoke a powerful energy that can serve as a source of safety, inspiration, and healing.

You, as an adult, can go back in time and offer the frightened child within the respect, love, safety, and comfort that was denied. Sometimes this kind of process can bring about an immediate release and relief. Sometimes it takes a lot of patience as the inner child develops enough trust to get in touch with feelings that have been too painful to feel for years. There may be many layers of feelings. First there may be fear, then anger, then layers of sorrow, and layers of shame.

Even if you don't feel like you can get into this inner child work by doing the exercises in this chapter, (whether it's because it doesn't feel like the time or place, or because it doesn't feel like something you want to try, or because this particular approach to inner healing isn't for you), appreciate yourself for being willing to read this chapter and consider what it says. Just thinking about the concepts here is likely to nurture self-understanding.

Joe At first I was skeptical of "inner child work" because I felt that I would not be able to relate to it in anyway. As we started the visualization process, I was instantly able to reach back into my past and discover some lonely and trying times. I was only able to reach back until the age of thirteen but reaching back that far as quick as I had, seemed to be a major start. In the visualization I was able to converse with my thirteen year old as if we were two people just hanging out. Actually, that's exactly what we were doing. I was able to sit down with my inner child and put my arm around him and talk about what he was feeling. He told me many things. I told him how much I understood and would help him in anyway I could. He told me of how he wished he had more support about decisions that he had made instead of no acknowledgment at all. I told him how he would now always have an arm around him and a shoulder to lean on in times of need. He immediately felt better about the situation and so did I.

As I continue to stay in touch with my inner child, the more relaxed the conversations seem to be. At first, it was as if my inner child and I were complete strangers to one another and didn't know how to proceed with conversations. We now have a good understanding of how we feel and it doesn't take a tremendous amount of effort for either of us to open up to one another. The tension has eased and when one speaks the other can almost finish the statement the other one started. I've learned that as a result of my inner child opening up to me, I can now open up to others without having to flare up. I am learning how to better cope with present situations in my life.

Re-Parenting Your Inner Child

In order to re-parent your inner child you will need to get in touch with the healthy adult within you. But, like many people, you may have never had any truly healthy role-models.

P A U S E   A N D   R E F L E C T

Since you may not have had models for a healthy adult, pause and reflect for a little while and imagine what qualities a healthy, loving adult would express. Some of the qualities might include: patience, a sense of humor, warmth, non-sexual affection, attention, sensitivity, protectiveness, respect, strength, emotional availability, playfulness, kindness, understanding, compassion, gentleness.

EXCERCISE

Exercise: Healing Your Inner Child

The following is a visualization to help you begin the process of healing your inner child. To begin this exercise it is important to relax. Find a comfortable position, relax your eyes, and take four or five slow, deep, relaxing breaths. As you breath out feel your whole body relaxing. Feel your breathing full and easy. Feel the weight of daily problems and demands slip off your shoulders for now.

If it's difficult for you to do this relaxation, I encourage you to jump ahead and read chapter nine first. Chapter nine gives specific directions on how to relax. Keep in mind that relaxation most often takes practice.

After the relaxation, you are invited to see yourself in the safest place you can imagine. This place will be different for everyone. It may be outdoors in nature. It could be a safe friend or relative's house from your childhood. It could be a real or imagined place of worship. Or a private room of your own creation that has all the comfort and safety you want. Your safe place may be different each time you do this exercise or it may always be the same.

If you have a tape recorder, you might want to slowly record the following visualization and play it back to yourself. If you are in a group that is dealing with the issues of emotional healing, you may wish to ask the counselor or group leader to read the visualization to the group. If neither of these are possible or desirable, you can read the directions over a few times and then just close your eyes, relax, and try to recall as much of it as you can. Or close your eyes after reading every three or four lines, letting go into your imagination as much as possible.

This kind of inner work can bring up powerful emotions. If it doesn't feel right to you to fully participate in the inner child exercises at this time, be gentle with yourself, and just read through them for now. If it feels right for you later, you can return to the exercises again, giving yourself the time and space to get into them at a more emotional level. Do what feels comfortable for you.

Also, rather than going back to early childhood right away, you can start by going back to later years first.

Healing your inner child is a process of letting him or her know that now there is really someone with whom their pain and innocence can be safely shared. This someone is the healthy adult within you.

To begin, find a comfortable position in a place where you are most unlikely to be disturbed. After you get comfortable relax your body. Take three or four deep letting-go breaths. Imagine breathing in a very soothing and peaceful energy and as you breathe out, feel yourself letting-go of tension and relaxing... Breathe in a peaceful energy. Breathe out tension. And with each breath allow yourself to feel even more relaxed.

Now see yourself in the safest place you can imagine. It can be a place you've been to before, or you can create such a place in your mind.

Imagine being in this place now.... Now imagine breathing in and out of your heart center. (The heart center is an energy center in your body near your physical heart, but in the center of your chest.)

With each in-breath, imagine breathing a gentle radiant light in through your heart center. As you breathe in this light, feel a peaceful radiance growing and expanding within you. As you breathe out, feel this radiance extending out into the safe place you are in. While you continue to breathe in and out of your heart center, allow yourself to open to feelings within you of gentleness and love.... Sense an inner strength deep within you. Sense an energy of gentleness and personal power within. (If you feel like you can't give your inner child this safety right now, or even if you feel you can, if you would like some extra love and support in this meeting, open your awareness and imagination and allow a loving guiding presence to join both you and your inner child. This guiding presence may take the form of a higher power, a spiritual teacher, or any being who you un-equivocally sense would be reliably loving, compassionate and totally protective. Allow this being to join you.) Don't judge what happens, just be as open as you can.

Now recall a time from your childhood when you felt frightened or unloved, a time when you were in need of safety and comfort, when no one was there for you.... Bring such a time to mind.... Where were you? Imagine that place again.... Was there any-one there?.... If so, who was it?.... See yourself as a child at that time.... Notice how old you were .... See what the world was like for you then.

Now imagine that this frightened child is with you right now. Imagine welcoming her/him with love and gentleness. Let the adult you with your present knowledge, wisdom, and strength be fully there for your inner child, offering her/him the respect, the comfort and the safety that was once denied.... Let her/him know that s/he is loved and safe now....

Imagine interacting with her/him. What does your inner child want or need to do now? Take your cues from her/him. Perhaps your inner child needs a hug, to cry, to be re-assured. Perhaps they need to yell or to tell you what has happened. Or perhaps they just want to play. Allow yourself to respond to her/his needs with compassion, wisdom, and total love... Open your heart and tell your inner child what s/he really needs to hear. Let her/him know that s/he is completely safe now and that you will protect her/him. Let her/him know that the unsafe past is over and that you will be there for her/him from now on.

Now imagine looking into her/his eyes, seeing and acknowledging your inner child's light.... Let her/him know that s/he always deserves to be loved.

(You could stop here in this visualization or go deeper by continuing on. Trust your instinct.)

If s/he wants to, allow your inner child to share their fears and pain with you. Listen as s/he tells you — verbally or non-verbally — the truth of their experiences, the truth of their feelings and painful memories....

Comfort her/him. Comfort her/him with your gentle, patient love and your heartfelt affection. Let her/him know that you will always be there. See your inner child responding, as s/he relaxes into the warmth and safety of your presence.

Imagine giving your inner child a special gift to remind them of your love and caring. The gift may be a toy animal to hold at night or a magical handkerchief to absorb any tears. It could be a punching bag to get out the anger that's been held in. Or it could be something else, perhaps even something you've never imagined before...... See her/him receiving your gift.... Imagine your inner child giving you a gift..... Imagine both of you experiencing a new bond, founded on love and forgiveness.....

Look into your inner child's eyes again and let her/him know that you will always be there for her/him as s/he grows into a strong and radiant adult. Make a promise to yourself and to your inner child that you will share time with her/him and give her/him the unconditional love s/he deserves. Make a plan with her/him to share some time everyday, even if it is just for a few minutes.... And now imagine your inner child gets smaller and smaller for now so that you can put her/him in your heart where you can be together. Take a few minutes now to reflect on your new connection and bond. Remember that your child is now safe and secure within your heart.

Come out of the experience in your own time. You may want to stay with the experience and think about it for awhile or you may want to move on.

* * *

In addition to this visualization, if you're willing, take some time each day to relax and get in touch with the adult you, with your present knowledge, wisdom and strength. Then share with your inner child, if only for a few minutes each day, offering her or him the respect, the comfort, and the safety that she or he may once have been denied. Listen to her/him. Nurture her/him.

EXERCISE

Writing To Your Inner Child

After you do or think about the visualization, take some time to write a letter to your inner child. Share your insights with him or her.

Tom

A letter to my inner child....

Dear Inner Child,

I always thought my childhood was pretty good. Then I contacted you for some clue to our past. After spending some time with you, much to my amazement, you told me some of the traumatic things that did happen to you when you were young. Please forgive me for not remembering them on my own. My mind has kept them well hidden for many years. I have only tried to remember the good things. You told me about the time when you were very young. The time when you had a cold and how your coughing disturbed Mom so much that she shut you in the spare room, in your crib, without heat, and closed the door, leaving you there so she could not hear your coughing anymore, and the pain, oh, the pain, jumping up and down crying please don't leave me here alone, I am frightened!

Then you told me about the time that your cousin, Russell, threw you up against a red hot, burning trash barrel and when you went upstairs Mom didn't want to be bothered because she was eating supper. Then you told me about the time that you broke your collar bone on the Tarzan swing and was so scared to go upstairs to show Mom that you sat on the next door neighbors step for an hour until you got up enough nerve to go up and tell her what happened. I didn't realize that these things still bothered you. I forgot that they even happened.

Well, things are going to be different now. I am going to be your Mother from now on! When I heard you crying, I went into that cold room and picked you up. I took you in my arms and said that I am here now and you will never be cold, alone, and crying again and that I loved you and would never let such a thing happen again! When you came up with that awful burn on your stomach, I dropped my food and took you in my arms again to ease your hurt and soothe your pain. I didn't blame you for what had happened. There would be time to eat later. Right now you are more important to me and again I told you how much I loved you and how sorry I was that you were hurt.

When I looked out the window and saw that you weren't in the back yard anymore, I went outside to look for you.. When I saw you sitting next door, I asked you what had happened and why you were crying? When you told me you were afraid to come upstairs to tell me I said that you don't have to be afraid to tell me and that it wasn't your fault that you broke your collar bone. Then I took you in my arms again and told you how much I loved you.

You will never ever have to be afraid again cause I am here now and I have felt the pain too. I will ease your pain and soothe you. I will give you lots of hugs and kisses. I will tell you every day just how much I love you and how important you are to me and that I can't live without you. I am here now and I will protect you from all harm. You will never have to be alone again.

With all my love,

Tom

Tom's Thoughts on His Inner Child

The last few days have been very busy for the two of us. I have found the friend that I never had — me. At first I didn't really think he was there but when I became aware of him I realized that he had been standing there all the time but I was ignoring him. He has a lot to say and I have listened intently to him. He is wiser than I thought. Now that I am older I can be what he needs to become what he wants. It's funny the things that I have noticed since we got acquainted. Everytime I heard a love song on the radio I would change the station because I have nobody special in my life and the songs would only bring sadness and remorse. Two marriages and two failures. He is trying his best to give me better insight as to why it happened the way it did, bringing me back in time, showing me how I didn't get much affection from my mother and comparing it to the relationships that I had as an adult.

What sticks out the most is what happened between my second wife and me. I was in the hospital, after an operation on my knee. I got a severe infection and was in tremendous pain. My doctor said that I almost died but the infection broke up all of a sudden. My wife came to see me twice. I was hospitalized for twenty-one days. Her reason was that our baby needed her at home and she did not want to get a baby-sitter. No wonder that our relationship went straight down hill from then on. Just like my mother putting me in that cold room, not seeming to care if I lived or died. She didn't want to be bothered with me.

Back to the love songs. Today when I heard those songs I sang them to my inner child and he sang them to me. I felt the love flowing between the two of us. I do have somebody special, real special. Somebody that I can love and somebody that can love me. It's like the beginning of a brand new life. It is the beginning of a brand new life!!

Andy

Dear Inner Child,

I have been running from you for most of my life. When you tried to express yourself, I would shut you out by intoxicating myself with alcohol or drugs, tucking you away so I wouldn't feel the fear, anger and shame that I felt when you tried to show yourself. When I try to escape from you by drinking and drugging I only get myself in trouble by committing crimes. I tried to hide from you by getting love and security from women but it didn't work. It seems like I'm always hurting myself. I think I always knew unconsciously that you was there but I did not know I was running from you. Now that I am facing the consequences of my actions, I realize that I must recognize you. I want to help you and get to know you better so we can help each other deal with our real feelings, become one, and get on with really living.

EXERCISE

Conversations with Your Inner Child

Another exercise you can do to interact with your inner child is to write out a conversation with your inner child using both hands. You as the adult will write with your dominant hand (the hand you normally write with). Your inner child will write or print with the other hand. Writing with your non-dominant hand may feel very awkward, but give it a try. Writing with the non-dominant hand helps you get in touch with parts of the unconscious that are not as readily available when you write with the hand you are used to writing with. You might open your conversation by telling your child you want to get to know her/him so that you can take better care of her/him. Ask for her/his name and anything else s/he wants to tell you about her/himself: age, how s/he feels, what s/he likes and doesn't like, what s/he wants from you, and how you can support her/him.

Your Inner Child and Your Children

Some parents can be there with a lot of love for their children even if they weren't parented with much love themselves. But often people whose parents couldn't show up for them aren't able to emotionally show up for their own kids. Active addicts, as much as they might like to think they are there for their kids, sell them terribly short.

One of the things that has been most striking for me is how after doing inner child work, after beginning to be there for their own inner child, people start being present for their own children as well. Sometimes people who have not had a relationship with their kids for years start reaching out with caring and love.

Mack stands out as one such person. When Mack was ten years old his mother put him under the custody of Youth Services in Ohio. Although his mother was quite comfortable financially, she didn't want to be bothered with Mack. She totally abandoned him and never went to visit. Mack went off on his own at eighteen. He got a job, got married, and had a child.

When his daughter was ten years old he left his wife and totally abandoned his child. He did to his daughter what was done to him at the same age. Now his daughter was about nineteen. It wasn't until Mack began to be there for his own inner child that he could mature enough to be there for his own daughter. When he could confront the rage of the child within him (instead of numbing it as usual), he felt enough strength and courage to be able to allow for his daughter's rage without shutting down and becoming defensive. When he began to develop patience for the hard work of his own inner healing, he developed the patience that would be needed as his daughter went through months and possibly years of developing trust for her father again. When he was there for his own inner child he became the man that his daughter needed.

Some people who haven't done "inner child work" begin to heal their own inner child through being a loving, patient, and understanding parent to their own child or some other child in need of a loving adult. Through being a loving parent, they naturally begin the process of healing their own childhood wounds.

If you are an addict, any time you indulge in your addiction you abandon yourSelf and your inner child completely (and everybody else that you care about.) You do what others have done to you before.

Being there with the warmth of compassion for your inner child and/or the emotions that have been frozen for years is the beginning of ending the cycle of lovelessness. With new awareness you can stop abandoning yourself like too many important people have done to you before. With compassion, patience, gentleness, and respect, turn and greet all of yourself. In this act, you release yourself and birth into your true power.

Ron My old tapes told me that I was not any good and never would be. I had tapes that were torturous to listen to. At least now I can entertain the thought of feeling some compassion toward myself and for that love starved, neglected little child that lives inside of me.

Today as a result of the this work I have begun to see, all be it faint, that beauty in myself and others and that means more to me than anything I have or will ever have. I can see the possibility of seeing the light inside myself and others, whereas before all I seen was the dark.

CHAPTER 5

Anger and Resentment: The Myth of Power

IF AS CHILDREN or young adults we were given some thoughtful and loving guidance about how to deal with our anger, I'm sure there would be far fewer prisons or prisoners today.

Anger isn't a problem in and of itself. It's a human emotion that everyone feels from time to time. It can be positive in that it may be a signal to us that something is unjust or threatening, that we need to pay closer attention to what's going on and, if necessary, stand up for ourself or others. Yet, in truth, people get angry much more often than is necessary and stay angry much longer than really serves them.

As we all know, probably too well, anger is a very powerful emotion and often an explosive one. When we have a lot of anger and we haven't learned to deal with it in healthy ways, one of three things happens. Either the anger gets directed outward as aggression, hostility, and sarcasm. In its extreme it comes out in raging, abusive, manipulative behavior. Or the anger gets turned inward as depression, a lack of motivation, self-abuse, and self-hatred. Or the anger gets expressed in what is often referred to as passive-aggressive behaviors like acting warm one moment and cold the next; being stubborn; routinely showing up late or ignoring and forgetting things; getting a partner sexually excited and then quickly meeting one's own needs and then physically and emotionally shutting down. These are ways of saying "F _ _ _ you" to yourself and others with a degree of anger that is most often not in keeping with the situation at hand.

Anger Triggered From the Outside

Let's take a look at some situations which might make you angry and how you might respond.

Someone steps in front of you in line. For no apparent reason, someone threatens you or pushes you on the basketball court. A rule gets changed for some seemingly ridiculous reason, and now you're confined to your cell for longer hours. A family member or a friend who promised to get you something has been too busy or forgot for the third time. Clearly things are always happening on the outside that can easily get you angry — things that you didn't ask for and things that you didn't provoke. Being human you find yourself getting angry when they happen. As long as you interact with others (and this is intensified in prison), situations that can potentially get you angry will present themselves again and again.

How you react, whether you quietly simmer with anger, blow up, or respond in a way that doesn't allow the situation to get the best of you, has a lot to do with the length of your emotional fuse. The more centered you are, the longer your fuse, and the more you are able to see what's going on. There's Steve doing his 'big bad wolf number." There's Bess playing out her "control act" again.

Seeing what's going on doesn't mean you won't get angry. But rather than blowing up within a fraction of a second, you have the awareness to see what your options are. Do you want to play at their level? Do you want to call him or her on what they're doing without getting pulled in? Do you want to fight? Is it worth risking the loss of good time, being locked down, or stopped from seeing your kids who are going to visit in three hours? Do you want to walk away? Do you want to stay on the court, let it go, and move on with the game? The more in touch you are with yourSelf, the longer your fuse, and the more likely you are to make choices you'll feel better about and won't regret later.

Reframing, relaxation, and meditation, which are taught in chapters eight, nine and ten, are all invaluable for adding inches or even miles to your fuse.

Unresolved Anger

When you read about making the choice to stand back in a situation where you find yourself getting angry, you may think this might be a reasonable approach for someone else but unrealistic, and perhaps even ridiculous, for you. When you think of situations that get you angry in your life right now, rather than seeing options, perhaps all you see is red.

If you have a very short anger fuse, you may think you are reacting only to the situations that are currently happening, but you are not. You are more likely spilling over with unresolved and buried hurt, sadness, and anger of many years — perhaps even a lifetime.

If you grew up in a family with alchoholism or any neglect or abuse, the old anger keeps playing itself out until the hurt and anger from the past are dealt with. It is an unavoidable consequence of growing up with so much aggression and/or disappointment.

Anger that is easily triggered *and* that is uncontrollable or explosive is rarely a fresh response to the situation at hand. Consider a situation when someone calls you a name and you explode into a rage. A reaction like this is likely to be the result of anger that has been stored up inside. If, for example, your father slapped you around, hit you with his belt, and put you down and you couldn't do anything about it, old unexpressed rage at your father might surface in any situation where you feel wronged or intimidated. You may be totally unaware of what's going on. As far as you're concerned, the person who called you a name deserves to be knocked across the room. Repressed anger is like a bomb waiting to go off, a short fuse waiting to be lit. If there isn't anger already boiling below the surface, you might get angry but you aren't likely to feel driven to act so aggressively and you can more easily let go.

How you were treated while growing up and what you learned from others about how to handle anger has a profound impact on how you deal with your anger now.

PAUSE AND REFLECT

Take some time to think (and if you are willing, to write about) each of the following questions.

- *How did your mother express her anger? What did she do when she got angry?*
- *How did your father express his anger? What did he do when he got angry?*
- *What did other important adults in your life (grandparents, aunts, uncles, teachers, older siblings) do when they got angry?*
- *Do you deal with anger like any of these people?*
- *How were you disciplined as a child? How were you punished?*
- *Did you ever feel in fear for your life?*
- *When you were a child and a teen, how did you express your anger? What did you do when you were angry?*
- *How did others respond to you when you acted that way? Did people care about the way you were feeling? Did you get any comforting? Did you get beaten, rejected, put down?*
- *Did you ever feel that your father would kill or seriously hurt your mother? Did you feel guilty? How did you cope?*
- *Did you have parents who expressed their anger in ways that felt safe?*
- *Do you feel you have a lot of anger?*

- *What do you do when you get angry now?*
- *Does what you do when you are angry usually lead to some kind of healthy resolution or does it seem to lead to more problems?*
- *Do you hold on to anger over long periods of time?*
- *How do you feel now about being hurt in the past?*

These may be difficult questions to answer. Answering them may bring up anger for you now. Try to be totally honest with yourself while noticing your responses with a gentle, non-judging awareness. Being aware and honest about your feelings will bring you increasing emotional freedom from negative events of the past. Becoming aware of what influenced you gives you the opportunity to step out of the unconscious reactions that undermine your inner peace and true power now.

Hector When I was growing up my parents taught me not to show anger. If I had showed any anger at any time I would have been beat up. So I was wise to keep my anger inside and never to talk about it. The way I got my anger out was by cursing my parents out in silence or sometime taking it out on my brothers or cousins. As I got older, withdrawing from everyday problems, from everybody and using drugs were others ways of coping with it.

Under the Anger

Actually, anger is a superficial feeling. By superficial, I don't mean that it is trivial or unimportant. I mean it's really only the tip of the iceberg. Many times we focus all our attention on our anger, not realizing that there are many feelings that are going on for us right below the anger at the same time. Because anger is often the emotion that speaks the loudest and demands our energy the most, it gets all of our — and others — attention.

PAUSE AND REFLECT

Pause for a few minutes and think back to a time when you felt angry. Try to get in touch with what was going on and how you actually felt at that time. Or, if you are currently feeling angry, pause and become aware of how you're feeling now.

Now take a deep breath and go deeper into your feelings. What's going on underneath your anger? Were you or are you feeling scared? Sad? Insecure? Helpless? Powerless? Hurt? Abandoned? Were you or are you feeling the disappointment of unmet expectations and unfulfilled dreams?

Look even deeper. Underneath the fears, frustrations and/or sadness, were you or are you asking someone to really listen and pay attention to you? Were you or are you, consciously or unconsciously, calling out for respect, acknowledgement, safety, caring, or love?

If you get lost in anger, you become deaf to your deeper feelings. In order to heal your anger you need to start listening, with an open mind and heart, to the deeper thoughts and feelings that lie beneath the surface as well. Most of the time the roots of anger can be found just before the anger arises. In all likelihood, just before you get angry, you are feeling frightened, or hurt and in pain.

The next time you get angry, see if you can become aware of the feelings that came before the anger or that are below the surface. If you can't step back at the time of the incident, then reflect on the experience later. You might want to return to the "Pause and Reflect" you just did. If you meet these feelings with respect, you can then deal with the situation more honestly and work it through in a way that is less apt to lead you to more of the same.

At times anger may be your safest response at first. But if you get lost in the anger you will see nothing else. Strong feelings require some unraveling to be understood. When anger or any strong feeling is being fully experienced, it interferes with clear thinking and logical reasoning.

And when we don't resolve anger, it often goes underground, quietly and persistently expressing itself as chronic resentment. Resentment is the feeling of grievance or ill will that lasts long after the situation that provoked the anger is over. Perhaps even long after a person you've been angry at has died. In resenting, you feel anger toward events that have been over for months or years; or worse yet, about things that have not even happened but that you only imagine might happen. Resentment is like holding on to burning wood with the intention of throwing it at another, all the while burning yourself.

Facing and Owning Your Anger

Many people have no problem getting angry. They carry their anger to the extreme and become "rage-aholics," spilling their anger out inappropriately with little or no regard for others. But there are others who, although they may have a great deal of anger, aren't consciously aware if it. Or they know it's there, but they keep it stuffed way down. In order to be emotionally healthy, people who stuff or deny their anger, need to deal with their anger as much as the people who vomit it on everyone.

If you are someone who rarely gets angry (1) because you learned to be that way when your anger was not tolerated as a child and you had to hold it in to survive, or (2) because anger was so destructive in your family and led to so much pain that you vowed (perhaps unconsciously) never to get angry yourself, or (3) because you had no healthy role models for expressing anger, then part of your healing includes giving yourself permission to feel the anger that has been pushed down or denied. We have to face and own our anger and pain, without judging it, in order to let it go.

This doesn't mean you should now get angry and dump your anger on others. This also doesn't mean directly confronting those who have hurt you or treated you unfairly, unless it feels like the right thing for you to do. But it does mean that the anger and pain that have been silenced need to be given the voice they were once denied. Then they need to be heard. The anger and pain need a safe witness, whether that witness is a counselor, clergy, a good friend, yourSelf, or, if you feel a connection, to God or a higher power. You can't get beyond your anger if it is in you and you haven't gotten to it yet.

For some people, it's easier to feel sad, depressed, and numb than it is to feel angry. If you are like this you probably had to stuff your feelings because there was no one safe who would listen. In fact, your anger might have been met with even greater anger by a parent or other adult. Anger may bring back memories of fear and pain. So, in order to avoid the pain, many people medicate their anger away. Smoke some dope, have a drink, snort some coke, mellow out. The problem with this is that the anger and pain don't get acknowledged and heard, and therefore don't go away. Just like anger and pain that are consciously pushed down and denied, anger and pain that are chemically numbed often return to haunt us in the form of depression or out-of-control rages that end up hurting us, others we care about, or people we don't even know.

Feeling angry may empower you to stand up for yourself and for the wounded child you were who couldn't stand up for himself or herself before. If you were denied your true feelings before, feeling angry now may give you the courage and power to stand up for yourself as you learn that you do indeed have a right to feel angry and assert yourself with anger, if needed. Often people who stay in abusive relationships have never learned that it is okay to feel angry and assert themselves. If you were physically or sexually abused as a child, feeling anger may be a crucial part of the process of taking back your body as your own, and asserting personal rights and clear boundaries.

It is important to feel the anger that has been denied and channel it in healthy ways.

Releasing It Safely

Some people are afraid to face their anger because they fear if they did, they might lose control. That's what they saw other people do. They may feel that they have so much anger inside that they could and would destroy the world if they let themselves really feel it. So they keep the lid on tight. There is a tremendous amount of energy in this anger. And it really won't go away by ignoring or pushing it all down, even though it may seem that way at first. If you have a lot of anger, it is important to channel that energy in as many healthy ways as you can.

These are some ways to channel your anger constructively. One is physical releases: Run. Lift weights. If there is a punching bag, let yourself get into punching it. Play any kind of sport. Games like racquetball or basketball that require a lot of energy are great outlets for releasing some steam. If you are confined to your cell, do push-ups or sit-ups. Even take a towel and twist it as hard as you can.

As you're running, lifting weights, punching the bag, or twisting a towel, you could even say "I'm angry, I'm angry" — over and over and over and over for three or four minutes. Don't get into a story about your anger. Don't say "I'm angry" at a particular person. Just keep repeating as intensely as you can get away with, "I'm angry." Acknowledge your anger. Let the energy of anger out.

Write about your anger. Give your anger a voice in writing. Write everything you are angry about. Keep writing until you feel you have gotten all your thoughts and feelings down on paper.

Talk your anger out with a trusted third party. Talk it over with someone you can safely share your true feelings with — someone who will listen without judging.

You *can* let that energy out in a way that is safe and won't hurt you or anyone else.

It may take days, weeks or months to work through some of your anger. Be gentle with yourself and respect what you need as you take this important step. It is also important to bring a great deal of awareness to the process of working with your anger so as not to get stuck there and let anger become a trap. If anger is within you, you need to feel it in order to let it go. If, however, you get stuck in always feeling angry or always needing anger in order to set boundaries, then the anger which is necessary at first to empower and heal you eventually disempowers you and inhibits your healing.

What Do You Get Out of Holding On?

Many people have no interest in working through their anger and resentment. For many of us there are major stakes in letting go of them because we get something out of holding on. We might get to control others with our anger. The increased energy and the adrenaline rush that can come with intense anger can give us the feeling of being more powerful. If we don't feel powerful or in control without anger, then of course we'll use anger as a favorite prop and defense. When we don't know how to hold our ground or get our point across without getting angry, then anger can serve as our security. A part of our mind might like to let go of the anger knowing, at least at some level, that we'd feel a whole lot better if we could let go. But until we find other emotional responses to the world that allow us to feel at least as secure as we do when we're angry, we'll keep reacting in old angry ways.

PAUSE AND REFLECT

Reflect on whether you use anger or resentment in any of the following ways.

- *Do you get angry because it gives you a feeling of being more powerful and in control?*

Anger may serve as the protection you need. If you grew up in an environment where people abused you and took advantage of you, getting angry might have been the one way to assert some power. Using anger to show your power may feel particularly necessary in some prison situations where others might test you with intimidation. Here your anger may indeed serve to protect you and help you establish your ground. If you sense that anger is the only language that someone will understand, then clearly an angry response makes sense.

But much more often than not, anger may be our response because we haven't learned to stand firm in our Self, to see the real dynamic that is going on, to call a spade a spade (speaking directly to the person we're dealing with, if necessary), or to walk away and not get hooked into the ego game that is probably going on. As mentioned before, up to this time anger may have been the best way you've known to demonstrate power, strength, commitment, and personal pride. And it may have served you well until this time.

But in fact, anger and resentment usually mask feelings of fear, helplessness, disappointment, or insecurity. Most often, anger and resentment are used as substitutes for feelings of genuine personal power.

As you pay attention and become more aware, you will certainly continue to get angry at times, but you will increasingly find yourself exhibiting your power and holding your ground not by a demonstration of anger but by the very power of your presence.

When you do get angry, be gentle with yourself. And when you're ready, look to see what you might learn from the situation. Given a similar situation, how might you respond to it differently? Look to see if there is a way that you could have asserted your power without getting or staying mad.

• *Do you use anger as the impetus and fuel for getting things done?*

Some people believe that if they didn't get angry then they wouldn't stand up for themselves or work for social or political change. Clearly anger can be and is often a positive motivator for change. It might be the fuel that one needs to get out of an abusive relationship or stand up for what is needed. There have been reforms in prison because inmates rose together in anger against inhumane conditions. Mothers Against Drunk Driving (MADD) was started by a woman who said she was so angry about the death of her child that she had to do something. Child labor laws, getting the right to vote, and many other positive social changes have come about as a result of people being angry about situations that were inhumane or unjust.

Yet anger does not have to be the only, or the primary, or, for that matter, any of the motivation for change. When we are in touch with our own true nature, with our empathy and inherent sense of fairness and justice, we can be moved to take action with passion and conviction. In many circumstances, when anger is the primary motivation for change, it elicits fear and generates resistance to the very change we are trying to make. And then instead of using our anger, we end up getting used by it.

• *Do you use anger to control others?*

Clearly, hostility, aggression, and anger can get others to feel so frightened or guilty that they can be controlled and manipulated. But as with all the so-called "benefits" of anger, you pay a high price in the process. The person who uses this tactic demeans and diminishes him or herself much more than the person being controlled. It is a power trip and like all power trips, it is used when one feels out of control and powerless inside (even if it doesn't appear that way).

If you use anger to control others, first acknowledge, without beating yourself up, the truth of doing it. Look back over your life and recall when you were controlled by intimidation and anger. Get back in touch with how you felt at those times. Really recall what it was like. Then breathe deeply, look into yourself, and see how you can show up with the integrity to not use anger as a way to control others in your relationships now.

- *Do you use anger to avoid communication?*

If you are afraid of taking the risk of being really honest with someone, if you are afraid of the possible consequences of your honesty, then you might use anger a way to avoid the truth. Anger distances us from others and may feel safer than intimacy and genuine communication. Think about various people you are angry with and then think about what you might risk if you were really honest with yourself and them.

If you stay angry in a relationship, there's not a lot of room for honesty. There's not enough safety for either person to get in touch with, and share the feelings under the tip of the iceberg. You may not have to face the truth of a relationship being over (even if it's still going on) or face the truth of how you really feel. Think of someone toward whom you are angry, and then go deeper to see and acknowledge the whole range of your thoughts and feelings in relation to this person. What would it be like to communicate the entire truth to them? If it feels right, perhaps you can try sharing it with them soon.

- *Do you use anger to help you feel safe? Does it seem to serve as a protection?*

When anger is projected toward others, they will often stay away. Using anger for self-protection may have been very creative and necessary when you were younger. And in a situation where you are really threatened now, anger is certainly a reasonable, understandable, and sometimes even necessary response. Again, if it is the only language someone responds to, then you need to speak it. But, as an adult, it is possible in most circumstances to set limits without getting and staying angry. First, you need to get clear about what is acceptable and unacceptable for you. Then you can set (or learn to set) limits with people who might try to disempower or dominate. If you have had a history of being dominated by someone, it is crucial to get support in learning to effectively stand up for yourself.

- *Do you use anger as a way of asserting that you are "right"?*

You may be thinking as you reflect on this question, "You'd better believe it! I am right, and she is wrong!" Releasing your anger does not imply that you are now acknowledging that the other person is right or that you are now wrong. Rather it teaches that "there is another way of looking at the world." You just see things as they are. If a person is wrong, they are wrong. You don't have to hold onto anger and stay miserable to prove the point.

- *Do you hold onto anger to make others feel guilty?*

If you are angry you may want to punish the person towards whom you feel angry. Reinforcing their guilt feelings is one way to do this. The major problem with this strategy is that as we do this, we simultaneously — although not consciously — reinforce our own guilt and unhappiness as well.

- *Do you use anger to avoid the feelings that are under the anger?*

As mentioned before, sometimes it's much easier to feel

angry than it is to feel feelings like fear or sadness that are under the anger. If we have learned to deny our feelings, acknowledging the feelings under the anger can be painful. But on the other side of the pain is relief and greater peace of mind.

In more extreme situations, when one is faced with an ongoing injustice or a profound personal violation like rape or the murder of a family member, until one feels more empowered and has some time and space to heal, anger can serve as a buffer from falling into hopelessness and deep despair.

- *Do you use anger to hold onto a relationship?*

As long as you are holding onto the anger, you are in a relationship with the person you are angry with. Anger is a commitment. Hatred is a commitment. If you are angry you need to ask yourself if this is the kind of commitment you really want to make. Many times a man or woman gets divorced in order to get away from his or her spouse. Yet as long as they hold onto resentment, they remain bound to the person they resent.

It may feel safer to hold onto the resentment than to let go because letting go may seem unbearably lonely or scary. This may feel particularly true in prison where the opportunity to get into new relationships with the opposite sex are few and far between for most inmates. When you harbor resentment it is as though you have a handcuff around your wrist and the other side of the handcuff is bound to the wrist of the person you resent.

- *Do you remain resentful, so that you don't have to take responsibility for your role in what's happening in your life now or how you feel?*

This may be one of the most powerful "benefits" of holding onto resentment. For as long as we hold onto resentment we can blame someone else for our unhappiness. It's somebody else's fault. This doesn't mean that others aren't at fault or that they don't contribute to our happiness or unhappiness, but even if we have been wronged, ultimately we are responsible for how we feel. If we indulge in recurrent resentments, we abandon the power we have to affect our own peace of mind.

Chronic anger diverts us from the understanding that regardless of our current relationship with the people who originally provoked our anger, if we continue to carry it around with us, we are now responsible for holding onto it or for choosing to let it go and moving on with our life.

• *Think of situation or person that evokes anger and resentment for you. Pause and ask yourself, "What do I get out of holding onto the anger and resentment?" Complete the following:*

What I get out of holding onto anger is _____.

What I get out of holding on to anger is_____.

What else I get out of holding on to anger is _____.

What I get out of holding on to resentment is _____.

And what else I get out of holding on to resentment is ___.

What I give up by holding on to anger is _____.

What else I give up by holding on to anger is _____.

And what else I give up by holding on to anger is_____.

Not only do we get something out of holding on to anger but we give up a great deal as well. You give up happiness. You give up peace. You give up personal freedom. And most importantly, you give up love. If you think these aren't possible anyway as long as you are in prison (or even if you are out of prison), know this is your ego and the popular culture talking to you. Although these negative voices are always there clamoring for your attention, as you commit yourself to knowing your cast of sub-personalities, honoring your feelings, and listening more deeply to yourSelf, you will find that peace, personal freedom, and love are where you are. The ego and popular culture will never give you peace and freedom, and when you listen deeply and own what is yours already, they can not take it away.

PAUSE AND REVIEW

1. Anger is normal and occasionally useful.

2. Anger can become a tyrant. It can run our lives by dominating the rich variety of feelings which we are capable of. And it can (and will) limit life choices.

3. In order to become free and truly powerful, we must debunk the myth of anger as power. We must move beyond the anger and resentment from our past and become more aware of the role that they play in our present.

4. We need to acknowledge both the anger and the feelings under the anger.

5. Then, get the anger out in healthy ways.

6. Ultimately though, if we want to live with peace of mind, we always need to let the anger go.

In chapter thirteen we'll explore letting go of anger towards others by forgiving, and in chapter twelve we'll explore healing the wounds inflicted by the most destructive anger of all, anger toward oneself.

CHAPTER 6

Grief: The Silenced Emotion

THE SCOPE AND depth of loss for prisoners is enormous. Just think about some of the most obvious losses you have had since coming to prison.

- the loss of the freedom to go about your life in the outside world
- the loss of the freedom to make hundreds of decisions a day: where you go, when you can move about, what you can eat, who you can visit, when you can make a phone call, where you work and what kind of job you can get (if any). In some situations it's as basic as losing the freedom to go to the bathroom when you want to (or need to).
- the loss of family and friends who no longer keep in contact now that you are in prison
- the loss of sharing daily life with a mate
- for most inmates, the loss of the opportunity to develop new friendships with people outside of prison
- the loss of being with your children as they grow up; the loss of the opportunity to take a more active role in their life
- the loss of sharing hundreds of special occasions with family and friends (holidays, birthdays, anniversaries, weddings, graduations, and funerals)
- for many inmates, the loss of a shared sexual life
- the loss of friends you make in prison who get transferred or released while you are left behind
- the loss of choice in medical and dental care (and, usually, the inability to obtain high quality care)

- the loss of material things
- the loss of privacy
- at least when one first comes to prison, the loss of remnants of self-esteem. The loss of a sense that you matter
- the loss of dreams
- and (in the U.S.A.) with greater and greater frequency, there is for some the ultimate loss, that of the right to live

Getting in touch with the profound loss and sadness that results from going to prison, especially if you are in for a long time, is hard in a culture that has little compassion for the pain and suffering of prisoners. Unless you have a counselor who has helped you address the issue of loss, you may feel (even if it is unconscious) that you don't even deserve to feel the sorrow that comes with a pained and misguided life. Although it is understandable in many circumstances, prisoners are most often met with an angry public reaction like, "You deserve it." Or "You should have thought of this before," rather than with any compassion or understanding. Going to prison is a socially unacceptable loss.

Yet in order to heal, you must honor the losses that come with your incarceration, even if others don't. See if you can find someone who can compassionately and simply listen as you put your losses into words. If there is no one you can share with, then try writing about your losses with as much compassion for yourself as possible.

Like many of the issues involved in emotional healing, just looking at the issue of grief and loss takes courage. Rather than facing the sadness or sorrow that comes with many losses, we often mask these feelings. Denying grief, acting like nothing much has happened when loss occurs, is learned in all dysfunctional families.

Denial of grief is also a cultural phenomenon; An innocent person has their head blown off and the assault and profound loss to the family and community is minimized and treated as entertainment. In a single parent household, Mom or Dad is out fourteen hours a day working to make ends meet or 'doing their own thing', and the anxiety, loneliness, and grief of the child left alone is ignored. If someone dies we say their loved ones are "doing well" if they act like nothing has happened. We say they're doing terribly if we see them crying a lot.

Grieving, feeling sadness about our losses, is a natural and normal feeling. If we cut our finger, we'll bleed. If we lose someone or something that is important to us, if we are emotionally healthy, we'll feel sad. Sadness is the natural outcome of loss.

Whether we consciously acknowledge it or not, the denial and blocked expression of sorrow — like any blocked emotion — will present itself in another form. The sorrow can get masked as a physical symptom; masked in depression or other expressions of emotional distress like chronic anger and hostility, or unhealthy shame and guilt; it can get covered over by addiction; and sometimes it gets distorted into apathy, disguised by an "I don't care" attitude.

For some people, there is no acknowledgment of the significant crises and losses that have been experienced: Your father leaves when you are a child and no one really talks with you about it. A spouse leaves, and the person who is left behind numbs out with drugs, works ninety hours a week, or runs into another relationship. A gang member comes into prison and gets into another gang without seemingly missing a beat. Instead of dealing with the real feelings about what's happening, the pain is swallowed, and life goes on "as usual." The grief is absent. And, as a result, healing becomes impossible.

....

PAUSE AND REFLECT

What are the losses you have experienced since coming to prison? Make a list. Breathe, remember to be gentle with yourself, and if it feels safe enough, allow yourself to identify the feelings that these losses evoke. If you are willing, write about your feelings or draw some pictures that describe what's going on inside you.

When you have finished, look over the list and see if there are any losses that reflect unfinished business with people (i.e. parents, children, mates, old friends, victims.) Reflect on whether there is something you can do to come to greater completion or healing in these relationships. If there is, and if you feel ready, do what you can to resolve these issues for now. Remember to try to treat yourself with some compassion as you do this. Try to be a good friend to yourself.

Losses of a Lifetime

Although you may never have thought of it this way, if you grew up in a family or community where you were abused or unsafe, you have endured tremendous loss. You have had to deal with:

- the loss of a happy childhood,
- the loss of a certain childhood innocence,
- the loss of faith in your own goodness,
- the loss of self-esteem,
- the loss of being able to trust and view the world as a relatively safe place,
- the loss of a solid foundation for a good life.

Most likely you have experienced other losses as well. Among them might be:

- the loss of respect and certain opportunities in life because of prejudice and bigotry,
- the loss of friends and family members by death,
- the loss of special relationships that didn't work out,
- the loss of employment,
- the loss of material things,

- the loss of physical health,
- if you are in recovery, the loss of the object of your addiction.

Dealing With Loss

Dr. William Worden, a specialist on grief counseling, identified four "tasks of mourning" to deal with loss. Consider how each of these fits into your own life. You may find these steps useful in your own healing.

THE FIRST TASK: ACCEPTING THE FACT OF LOSS

The first task of dealing with loss is acknowledging your losses and accepting the fact of the loss. To name your losses and speak about them makes the losses "real." It means they are happening or have actually occurred. In many cases this may be extremely painful to deal with. In other cases, like the death of a person who has created a lot of aggravation or suffering for you, the loss may feel like a relief.

If it is a painful loss, we may get lost in anger and denial and run from the truth to shield the part of us that doesn't want to feel or believe that the loss is real.

Ralph The first loss that I had to accept was that I was in prison and there was nothing I could do about it. Accepting this, as obvious as it was, took in itself in excess of four years which included two years on the run, two years fighting in court, and one year in a state hospital before I was able to accept that I had to do this time and get it behind me.

In order to move on with life, like Ralph, we all have to come to accept the fact of loss, the meaning of it, and, in many instances, its irreversibility. Then, we can deal with the truth of our situation as best we can, and with patience and intention, work through at least some, and (depending on the circumstances) perhaps all of the pain.

SECOND TASK: MOURNING

To mourn our losses means to identify the feelings that are associated with the loss and to face our feelings openly, honestly, and with gentleness. All healing requires some compassion for ourself, truth-telling, and self-acceptance.

Grieving or mourning may ask us to accept a range of deep feelings. Sadness is just one. In mourning our losses we may experience feelings of helplessness. It can be painful and frightening to acknowledge how many things we have had (and have) little or no control over. Anger, guilt, shame, despair, love, compassion and passion may also arise. Author Clarisa Pinkola Estes writes of "Letting the heart break — not break down — but break open." If it opens, you will feel pain. And you find relief and renewal.

Crying is not always a part of grieving or mourning our losses, but if we are open and in touch with our deepest feelings of loss, there will, in all likelihood, be tears. Even outside of prison crying is very difficult for most men, as it is for women who have had to be tough and street-wise to survive. Childhood taunts and threats like "Cry and I'll really give you something to cry about;" "Crying is for babies and wimps;" or, "Be a man" all feed into a need to abandon true feelings and become un-real. As you know, crying in prison where any show of vulnerability is interpreted as a sign of weakness is, except in rare circumstances, totally taboo. It's understood, you just don't do it. Even in counseling groups that feel safe, there is the fear of being judged and perceived as weak or foolish. This is particularly true for men. Men are supposed to be "strong." "Men aren't supposed to cry." But pockets of safety where one can shed some tears and be real do exist and can be created.

Try to find a counseling situation or group where it is safe to be real. If there are times when there aren't others around and sadness comes up, without automatically putting the lid on your feelings, be gentle with yourself and give yourself some space to feel. If tears arise, cry into your pillow if necessary. There is an expression, "He who doesn't cry, doesn't get cured."

George For some reason I wasn't able to cry before. I've never been able to really cry but since this course I've done it at least 3 or 4 times. I've had a lot of hurt and pent up emotions. Couple of the other guys said the same thing. The flood gates were opening. It's like a release valve. It really hurts to feel some things at first but after you get into it and look at it, you feel a lot better.

A seventeen-year-old young man interviewed on a television talk show about why he abused his girlfriend put it this way: "Some people cry. If you can't cry, you strike out." When you push your real feelings down, they do a number on you. And they come out sideways. Instead of feeling the pain, you might (consciously or unconsciously) look for someone to pick on or abuse. You dump your pain on others. I'm sure if men (and some women) could cry more easily, there wouldn't be a fraction of the addiction and violence that there is in the world today. Hearts would not get hardened by unshed tears. We can be relieved by our tears. And contrary to what many think, we can be strengthened by them. In truth, your heart wants to cry for your losses. It wants to cry over what has happened. When it can't express itself, there is a grief overload. The grief might come out not only in striking out, but in insomnia, emotional numbness, ulcers and other physical symptoms, and as mentioned, depression.

PAUSE AND REFLECT

If you allowed yourself to experience the full pain of your losses, what do you imagine you would do and feel?

If you have kept your grief shut away, you probably did so because it felt like the safest thing to do. Like George — who began to cry for the first time in many years while participating in the Emotional Awareness/ Emotional Healing class — most people feel better as they allow themselves to feel the pain of their losses.

However, just as grieving can empower us, if it becomes extreme, it can be disempowering. Grief that is debilitating and prolonged may be a sign that we need help to resolve the losses. An example of this would be a person who is lost in grief about the end of a marriage many years after the marriage has ended.

Healthy grieving doesn't mean we won't hurt or ache again. The nature of deep grief is such that with certain profound loss, deep hurt, or harm we may never be done grieving — a life in prison, the loss of a child by death, the loss of one's own childhood through abuse. Although the grieving may bring true relief and emotional healing, and the periods of grieving are further apart and last for shorter periods of time, another layer of the grief may arise again. When this happens, the most healing thing we can do for ourself is be gentle and have compassion for our humanness.

In her book, *The Courage to Grieve* author Judy Tatelbaum writes, "Grief is a wound that needs attention to heal. To work through and complete grief means to face our feelings openly and honestly, to express and release our feelings fully and to tolerate and accept our feelings for however long it takes for the wound to heal. We fear that once acknowledged grief will bowl us over. The truth is that [a great deal of] grief [that is] experienced does dissolve. Grief unexpressed is grief that lasts indefinitely."

....

PAUSE AND REFLECT

If you face your losses openly and honestly, what are the feelings that arise? As you acknowledge these feelings, remember to be gentle with yourself and thank yourself for having the courage to reflect on your life in this way.

THIRD TASK: ADJUSTING TO THE NEW SITUATION

If we can acknowledge our losses and meet our true feelings about these losses with greater honesty and compassion, we clear the way to adjusting to the new situation as best we can. We can establish new roles and a new identity as way of healing. If you, for instance, came to prison an addict and now choose to use prison time as a time to heal, then by facing your losses, you are free to move out of the old identity and into the new identity as someone in recovery, someone who despite being in prison, is finding inner freedom and building a positive life. You can look to the future and see more of the possibilities that are there. You can let more of your true spirit come back into your life.

Ralph The next loss was that when my wife and child and family left. I believed so strongly that I needed them to survive that I literally began to deteriorate physically and emotionally until I was able to face the truth that I could have a life without them. That inside me existed a person who could stand alone and heal and ultimately achieve happiness.

FOURTH TASK:
INVESTING YOUR ENERGY IN SOMETHING NEW

After healing through some of your loss, the fourth task is to withdraw your investment in the people, roles, and things you have lost or given up and re-invest your energy in new things. Some people might decide that as a result of coming to prison the possibility of a meaningful life is over and, as a result, not invest their energy in healing and or anything positive and new. You may feel like you don't deserve a fulfilling and decent life if you have left a mess behind you. Or you may feel its easier or less painful to keep yourself from caring. It's hard to begin to put any value in life and faith in yourSelf when you never learned to before. But, don't give up. Don't stop living — even if you are on death row. Don't bury yourself yet. When you heal, you are never healed alone. By healing, you heal others. Give yourself permission to invest your energy into something positive.

As painful as the losses dictated by a prison term may be, for many people they represent an important step towards reclaiming a meaningful life. Without certain losses many people would not re-direct their lives in positive ways. As one inmate said, "I was so caught up in my life and as destructive as it was, I couldn't stop. If I didn't have these losses, I wouldn't have slowed down enough to heal." Because he actively invested his energy in facing and healing some of his horrendous childhood losses, he described prison as "the most painful and difficult thing" he had to endure, and yet, "the biggest gift."

Consciously dealing with loss enables you to unblock your heart so that the energy of compassion and wisdom can be more available to transform any situation you are in.

EXERCISE

Honoring Loss and Letting Go

Find a comfortable position and take five deep, relaxing, letting-go breaths. With each out-breath, remind yourself to relax. Imagine you are in a very safe place and that there is a light shining down on you that protects you and fills you with peace. Now allow someone or something that you have not yet let go of and said good-bye to — someone or something that is over and yet unfinished — come to mind. (It could be someone who is dead, someone who is alive, it could be your freedom to go about your life on the outside, it could be the object of an addiction, the old you.)

Put into words any feelings of anger, hurt, remorse, regret, understanding, gratitude.

If you are saying good-bye to a person, imagine that they are able to hear your message. Remember to breath and feel yourself bathed in light. If grief arises, let yourself feel it. Open your heart to yourself.

When you have finished, ask yourself if you can truly say good-bye and let go of the person or situation. When you are ready, see the person or thing leaving this safe place. Feel the light relaxing you and melting the barriers to your heart. Breathe in and feel the wholeness within your own being. After staying with this feeling for a while, when you are ready, gently return to a regular awareness.

I encourage you to return to this exercise often. Use it to deal with losses you have experienced in the past and ones that you will face in the future. Certain losses may be fairly easy to deal with, while others may take a long time. Try to be patient with the process.

PAUSE AND REVIEW

The four tasks of dealing with loss are (1) accept the fact of the loss; (2) mourn the loss. Identify the feelings that are associated with the loss and face them openly, honestly, and compassionately. (3) do what you can to adjust to your present situation. (4) give yourself permission to invest your energy in new and positive ways.

As long as you live, you will continue to experience one kind of loss or another. Each time you are able to honor the losses you endure, and experience the sadness and grief that follow, you are involved in healing. This is an ongoing task which demands strength, courage and compassion of you. It is an undertaking that will take you through to a new awareness of who you are and who you can become. Whenever you face the truth of your experience and let your heart break open, you will find that instead of losing heart, your capacity to feel justified hope will grow a little larger. Facing losses honestly, dealing with them consciously, opens the way to move on and make the most out of life.

PART 3

CHAPTER 7

Forgiving on Neutral Territory, or ... Learning to See

NOW THAT YOU'VE spent some time exploring your personal past and the feelings that go along with your experiences, we're going to lighten up. This chapter will introduce you to a powerful new way of living. I call this approach "forgiving on neutral territory" or "learning to see." This is not "forgiving" or "seeing" in the usual sense. Usually if we think about forgiving someone, a person we've been angry at will come to mind. Later in this book we'll look at the issue of forgiveness in this familiar way.

But first I want to encourage you to practice a form of forgiveness that you can use with people you aren't angry at or people you may never even have seen before. Understandably you may think, "then I have nothing to forgive them for." And, in the usual sense of forgiveness, you are right.

When I teach about forgiveness, I always start by extending an invitation to the people I am speaking with. I extend that invitation to you now. I invite you to pause for a minute or so and do the following:

In your imagination, take your hands and put them into your head. Then gently pull out all the ideas that you currently hold about forgiveness. Put these ideas somewhere they will be safe in case you want them later. Put all your old ideas aside for now and leave your mind open to a whole new way of thinking about what forgiveness is and how you can apply it in your daily life.

In chapter two I wrote about how each of us has a core Self, the part of us that is clear, peaceful, wise, and loving. And each of us has a personality or ego. Part of the nature of the ego is that it is always judging. It's like a judgment machine. It turns out one judgment after another. When we see or meet someone, without our conscious awareness, the ego often goes into action. We judge others by the way they look or act, or we judge them based on something we've heard about their past. We may judge them as cool, stupid, a jerk, or a _____ _____ (fill in the blanks) — or in any number of other ways. Without even knowing it, we've slipped into a robe and appointed ourselves Judge.

Do you ever notice yourself judging people you don't even know as you walk through the halls or hang out in the gym? Are there people you have pegged even though you haven't met them?

When we meet someone, within moments the ego often firmly establishes whether we should like the person or not. Then every future thought we have about this person or every future interaction with them is based on this decision that we made in the past. When we are confined to our ego, we are slaves to past perceptions. New insight and understanding have no place in our present.

Because the ego is always judging and comparing, it sets up a hierarchy which leaves us feeling inferior or superior to others. We either feel a sense of not being good enough or an inflated sense of arrogance or superiority. We think we are a better or a lesser person.

When we operate from our ego, we automatically look for what separates us and makes us different from others. The thinking might look like: I'm in here for this crime, you're in here for that crime. I'm in here, you're out there. I'm one race, you're another. I'm from one ethnic group, you're from another. I have a certain educational level, you have another. I come from this neighborhood, you come from that neighborhood. These distinctions are not seen as mere facts. We attach judgments to each of these distinctions. When we see through the eyes of the ego, we not only scan for the differences that separate us, we make value judgments about them. For example, you might see an inmate who reads all the time and keeps to him or herself. You don't know this person but you might judge him or her, deciding they're a wimp and not worth your time.

The Self sees from a fundamentally different vantage point. Rather than looking for what is better, worse, or different between you and others, it looks for what is the same between you and others. Whether we play different roles, or are a different sex, or have committed different crimes, or come from different backgrounds, or act in very different ways on a daily basis — we share something in common. At the core of both of us is a light. We both have different lampshades, yet we both have a core spiritual Self that is the essence of who we are.

When we practice forgiveness on neutral territory, as Dr. Jerry Jampolsky, the author of many books on forgiveness says, "We see the light instead of the lampshade in others." Actually, I don't see forgiving on neutral territory as "seeing the light (the Self) *instead* of the lampshade (the small selves)." I do see the lampshade, but I see it as only a small part of who a person really is. The ego would have us believe that there is nothing more than what we see through its' filter of judgment. The person is just a jerk, an idiot, a child molester, a white person, a woman, or whatever. That's it. Our ego would argue that there is nothing more than the lampshade, nothing more than what first meets our physical eyes.

The "light" in others can't be seen with our physical eyes. It is often buried under fear and acts of toughness, shyness, disrespect, etc. The only way to see that light, that core of sanity and goodness, is through the *willingness* and *intent* to see it. You have to create it out of what appears like nothing. You have to be willing to see through the eyes of the heart. Only the heart or the Self has the boldness and vision to see the light in another. Only the Self can see light through a veil of clouds. Only the Self can create and see what is not obvious to the physical eyes because the Self doesn't take things at face value.

EXERCISE

Seeing the Light

To begin the practice of forgiveness on neutral territory, I encourage you to do the following:

Take at least a few minutes, three times a day, for the next month, to practice "forgiving" or "seeing" with people you haven't met before or don't know well. Allow yourself to see beyond their outer appearances and see, instead, the Self— the light. In other words, inwardly acknowledge that each person you see has a peaceful, loving, and wise nature. You can do this as you walk down a hall, stand in a line, or anywhere when there are others around (or even in your imagination when there aren't others near by). No words or outer gestures are needed. Just a quiet inner recognition is sufficient.

As you see them remind yourself, "that person is, in essense, good, loving and wise, no matter what I see with my eyes."

* * *

To practice forgiveness in this way, you don't have to be actually looking at a person. Again, this is an inner process. You don't need to say anything or outwardly do anything. "Seeing" is just inwardly acknowledging that there is a core Self in another. It is the inner recognition that behind what meets the physical eyes, behind the acts and outer appearance, is a person of goodness and value, a person who, at the bottom line, wants what you want — to be safe and to be loved.

Author Hugh Prather says that "forgiveness is not some futile act in rosy self-deception, but rather the calm recognition that below our egos, we are all exactly the same." Below our egos we are calm, powerful, lovable and loving people. Again, it takes courage, willingness and intent to see this bigger picture.

In a book that I read many years ago, a student in his twenties went to Mexico to study with an old Indian wise man. The wise man tells this student that in order to see, truly see, he must be willing to "see the world beyond the description that he had learned to call reality." We are not talking small change here. We are talking "seeing the world *beyond* the description that we have learned to call reality." We have learned a description of the world based on the petty and limited perceptions of the ego. The ego always sees only part of the picture. It then mistakes a part of the picture for the whole picture. Big error! Yet it is the nature of the ego to see in this limited way.

By forgiving on neutral territory we become more aware and heal the habitual judgments and separation from Self that often pervades much of our thinking. We nurture the ability to see the whole truth of who we and others are.

In a sense, you are the object of millions of peoples' egos right now. People may not really know who you are but since you are a part of a group called "criminals," many people make numerous judgments about you. Some judgments may be accurate and many judgments that people assume are true about you may not have a thing to do with the truth. They don't really see you. They are lost in judgment and fear.

If one sees the whole truth about "prisoners" or "criminals" one recognizes that even though most men and women in prison are guilty of crimes, there is a fundamental innocence under the ego that once propelled their criminal behavior. Although most people in prison (and out of prison) are emotionally wounded in some way there is also wholeness and the potential for healing. There is an enormous amount of anger and rage in many prisoners from a past and present of being disempowered and demeaned within the family and society. Yet, if someone were to really see, they would find the potential for inner peace and true power. They would see the darkness created by fear as well as the light of the Self.

While walking down the street or facilitating a group in a prison, I often see the light and positive potential in others. The reason for this is simple. When I get up in the morning and as I go through my day I make the decision to *see*. I don't always see. Like anyone, I get caught up in fear and judgments of my own. But by "practicing forgiveness", by making it my intention to see with the "inner vision" of the Self rather than the "outer vision" of the ego, I *see* in more and more moments of my day. The more I see, the more peaceful and effective I feel. When I see the light in people I am interacting with, they often respond in a way that tells me that they feel more peaceful and empowered as well.

Seeing is like exercising a spiritual muscle. If I want my biceps to be larger, I lift weights. I exercise and with time my muscles grow. If I want to see the whole picture, really see, I exercise my spiritual muscles, acknowledging the light in others. I use the gift of inner vision that we are all given. I acknowledge the part that is always worthy of respect and love — even though my ego would like to disagree at times. My ego would assure me that some people don't have a Self, that the light of some people is definitely out. But, seeing with inner vision requires the willingness to choose my perceptions once again and acknowledge and trust in what may be completely hidden from view. Forgiving, in its most expanded sense, is a willingness to trust in the goodness and potential in another even though they may not even know or trust this power in themselves. Again, at a personality level, they may be so constricted and fearful that they are starkly disconnected from this reality.

When we meet someone, if we choose to acknowledge them, a common greeting is "hello." What are we really saying when we say "hello"? Usually we're acknowledging that there is a body and personality in front of us. In a South African culture when people greeted someone they would say, "Sawabona". This word translates into "I see You." Not, just I see your body or personality, but I see You. "You" with a capital "Y". I see your true Self, your fundamental goodness and innocence.

Imagine what your life might have been like if everytime someone greeted you, they said, "I See You", if everytime they met you, they affirmed your goodness, strength, and brightness.

FROM TIME-TO-TIME AS YOU GO THROUGH YOUR DAY
CONSIDER THE FOLLOWING:

I am willing to see.

Why Bother?

The practice of forgiveness on neutral territory gives you an incredible opportunity to observe your habitual judgments and the mind games the ego thrives on. It gives you the opportunity to take off the robes, relax, and take a vacation from the stressful, entangling, no-win job of being "the Judge." It frees you from getting so hooked into other peoples' acts. By seeing, you empower yourself not to let another person's sub-personalities and moods have as much power to determine your own.

If you don't know who others are, you don't know who You really are either. If you are judging others, you are lost out in your own small judging self. When you see others as small, you remain small. Your ego remains hooked into their ego.

If you are doing time, you get psychically bombarded by the message that you have anything but a peaceful, wise, and loving nature. Certainly you may have been very disconnected from this innate Self, but it is within you. And seeing it in others is a most powerful way to mirror your own true identity back to you. When you see the greater possibilities in others, you realize these possibilities in yourself. *Seeing the Self in another is a key to knowing who you really are. Each time you acknowledge the light in another, you affirm that reality in yourself.*

The ego is like a couch potato. It's used to lying around clicking in the same old programs. More of the same is all you'll find on these old familiar channels. To do this work you have to be willing to tune in to channels you may not even have known existed. Your ego will unquestionably resist at times. The nature of the ego is such that it isn't interested in change. It's invested in the familiar. It is into its old judgments. Conflict is its second name. And it will suck you back in every chance it gets. The Self, however, is yearning for change. It wants to taste freedom. It knows inner power and freedom are it's nature. It's tired of the same old show and it lets us know it by feelings of numbness and pain, chronic anger and distress.

With your willingness and intent to practice Seeing on a regular basis for a while, you will begin to tune into channels that you won't want to shut off. They will give you new insight and understanding. They will give you greater emotional freedom. They will give you back yourSelf.

Reflecting on Forgiving on Neutral Territory

As you go through your day, practice forgiveness on neutral territory. At the end of the day notice any reactions and insights you have about yourself or others as a result of practicing forgiveness on neutral territory. And complete the following incomplete sentences:

When I practiced forgiveness on neutral territory what I noticed about others was _____.

What I noticed about myself was _____.

The way I felt was _____.

The way I usually feel when I look at others is _____.

What I learned about myself and others is _____.

✳ ✳ ✳

Here is what some participants in the Emotional Awareness/ Emotional Healing courses found.

Ralph When I practiced forgiving on neutral territory what I first noticed about others was their outer appearance: Tough, Hard, Sad, Jokers. I noticed that others aren't as bad as I thought. I then began seeing their need for acceptance and love.

What I noticed about myself was the way I want people to see me. I keep my true self hidden.

The way I felt was phony. I felt fear. I want people to know and see the true self, but taking down the front is risky.

The way I usually felt about others was angry, fearful, judged, and disrespected.

What I learned about myself and others was we all are very much alike. We hide behind fronts or masks believing we are unacceptable as caring, loving, and valuable human beings.

Jack I just tried it a few times. There's a fear in forgiving people in this place. It comes with the territory. But I'll keep trying to forgive in small doses.

Lenny I've been going around the past few days looking at people differently. It wasn't uncommon for me to look at people and wonder what they are really like. Now I'm trying to do it with a few people here that my ego got the best of me on. I try not to judge but there are a couple of people here I didn't like although I've never spoken with them. I'd heard something about them. Something they said to my friend so I made up my mind what kind of person he was because of what he said. Now I'm trying to look past that, understand why he's like that.

One guy has a very angry sub-personality. I sat down and talked to him for a moment using the understanding I've gotten about forgiving so far. I got him to look under his anger towards his ex-wife. At first he made jokes but I'd say, "Seriously." Finally he started talking about the hurt and betrayal he felt, and the insecurity being 52 years old. In 3 years he'll get out and have to start over. I really didn't like this guy before. I'd hear him talking in the kitchen (we work there together) and I'd hear an old man trying to be big and bad. I had no desire to talk to him. He seems to have opened up to me a little and talks to me the way two people should talk without a sub-personality dictating his words. Now I see that a lot of his comments were an opening for attention and possible sympathy but I used it for an opening to get to know his Self and plant a few seeds so he might look at things a little differently. By the end it was like we were two different people. I found that I can understand others if I want to and that I'm no better a person or no worse than anyone else.

FROM TIME-TO-TIME REFLECT ON THE FOLLOWING:
There is another way of looking at the world.

CHAPTER 8

Reframing: There Is Another Way of Looking At The World

ALTHOUGH WE ARE NOT always aware of the connection, certain individuals and events are almost certain to trigger predictable reactions. Just the thought of a certain person may leave you feeling hostile. You may find yourself irritated every time you have to wait in line a little longer than you'd like. Cloudy days may leave you feeling down. We all have certain people and circumstances that *trigger* predictable thoughts, feelings and behaviors in us.

Of course positive feelings can be triggered as well. The thought of a special person in your life may leave you feeling more peaceful and loving. Since people or circumstances that we feel really positive about aren't as likely to leave us feeling stressed-out, we'll focus on the more challenging circumstances here.

....

PAUSE AND REFLECT

Fill in the blanks.
_____ *makes me angry.*
I can't stand it when _____.
Every time I think of _____ *I feel* _____.
When I think of _____ *I feel* _____.

I get upset when _____.

....

As you go through your day, watch the things that you react to. Pay attention to what triggers you as you walk down the hall, stand around in the gym, in the visiting room, in the library, in your room or cell, or anyplace else.

Ramon   As I reflect on my day the things that triggered me were waking up and realizing that it's another day that I have to spend in jail. As I walk in the hallway towards the chow hall I notice that what triggers me are the CO's giving us their killing stares. While I wait in line for food the thing that triggers me is the kind of food that they serve in here. In the gym the camera is what triggers me. I notice that anger and frustration are the emotions that get triggered the most.

Who's Doing What To Whom?

As you observe yourself, you will begin to see a connection between certain people and circumstances, and your moods and emotions.

Even though people or circumstances *may trigger* certain thoughts, feelings and behaviors, they *don't have to determine* your thoughts, feelings or behaviors. You don't have to stay stuck in anger, fear, or upset. In fact, when you stay stuck you are, in a sense, giving over your power to that person or circumstance. Say, for instance, a staff person has a history of putting inmates down. One day you see this person and he interacts with you in a way that seems insulting. His behavior triggers a lot of anger in you. Your blood pressure rises, and, for the next five hours, you are quietly fuming and wishing you could get revenge. You're impatient and negative with most everyone else who you interact with for the rest of the day. This includes a friend who comes to visit.

If you think about this situation, *you are giving* this staff person *the power* to insult you and rob you of inner peace. You are handing over to them the power to determine how you feel. It's as if you silently say to him, "Here's my inner peace. Here's my power. Here's my well-being. I give control of my feelings to you." That's a lot of power to give someone!

Our ego often justifies this kind of reaction with thoughts like "They *make* me mad." "They piss me off." When in truth, they don't make you mad or pissed off. If you are an adult, people can't *make you* feel anything — unless you let them. You hold the power for your inner state — unless you give it away. You give a situation the meaning it has for you.

Do you see these people as someone who is abusing you *or* do you see them as people who are separate from their Self, people who are lost in their own sub-personalities? If they regularly put others down, whether they are staff, inmates, or anyone else, do you see them as total jerks, as people to get *and stay* angry at *or* do you see them as people who are insecure and have to put others down to have the illusion of raising themselves up?

The way you see them is a choice. And your choice determines whether you will feel victimized by them or see what is really going on and as a result feel secure within yourself. In truth *it isn't really a person or circumstance that causes your reactions; rather, it is your own thoughts and attitudes about this particular person or situation that are the source of your stress.*

If you take the demeaning behavior in the above scenario personally rather than seeing that this person is just doing his number again, then of course you'll get pulled in.

We all react to others at times, but the more aware we become, the less time we spend wasting our energy in this way. When we see clearly, we take back responsibility for our own well-being rather than getting hooked in and then blaming our unhappiness on others. Richard's experience is a good example.

rd Today my impatience was triggered by an inmate who
d me to explain how to study the chapters in a course we are
taking. He started to yell at me for not listening to his opinion about
a certain matter. I saw myself starting to yell back but I became
aware of my reaction and stopped and said, "If you want me to help
you, you're going to have to stop yelling. I spoke softly and said I
wasn't willing to get into a yelling match. I stayed in mySelf and he
calmed down, so instead of our sub-personalities going at it we
talked Self to Self. I taught him for an hour. He later came back into
my room and thanked me for being so patient with him.

Richard's impatience got triggered but rather than getting stuck
there, he became aware of his reaction and choose to respond differently. But sometimes the situation won't resolve itself as easily or
as well as this one. You may be dealing with someone who is out of
control or into a major power trip.

Clearly there are people who have (or act out) a certain kind of
outer power. Anybody who is or has been victimized knows this all
too well. If you are in prison you certainly know this. Even so you
have a choice: do you want to empower the person who had (or has)
the outer power further by giving them the power to determine your
level of inner peace and well-being indefinitely?

If not, you'll need to step out of a familiar dynamic:

1. First, you have to become aware of your emotional reaction.
The moment you become aware of it, you are no longer lost in it. In
your own mind, think of a situation where you feel triggered into
anger, frustration or irritation by another person. Imagine this situation and imagine being in it, yet, at the same time, emotionally
stepping back. Become an observer of what goes on. Watch your
reactions *without judging* them.

2. Notice how this person is identified with his or her sub-personality, for instance "The Intimidator," "Tough Girl" "I'm Better
Than You" "Irresponsible." Notice how the person is separated from

their Self. A person in touch with Self certainly wouldn't be acting this way.

3. Notice your judgments about them. Notice how your sub-personality is hooking into their sub-personality.

4. Affirm to yourself:

> *I can see this situation clearly now.*
> *I can choose to be more centered, calm, and clear.*
> *The power of decision is my own.*

5. Look to see if your own behaviors and attitudes contributed to this situation, and if they did, imagine taking responsibility for yourself.

If you feel that you can't choose to be " more centered, calm, and clear" in the particular situation you are in, be gentle with yourself. Thank yourself for even contemplating this possibility! Even if you don't experience an inner shift in that situation, your expanding awareness of the choices you have in relation to how you respond will increasingly empower you to be more peaceful and less at the effect of other potential stresses.

Theo First it should be said that I hold no prejudice against any human being. I have had my share of problems in life and I don't see any justice in creating problems for others. It makes no difference what the color of a persons skin is, their sexual preference or any of a variety of differences that prove us to be unique individuals.

I have made friends with many people during my stay here in prison. The most controversial of my friendships is with a young man that is gay. I am heterosexual and receive a lot of flack because of my friendship with this young man. I can deal with the hordes of idiots that crawl out of the woodwork to verbally assault me. In other words, I can hold my own. But when I find this assault being thrashed upon my friend I become so angry that I find myself preparing to fight.

Tonight there was an incident provoked by many. As my friend and I stood outside of my cell talking, a young man decided to try and embarrass my friend by coming out of the shower in the nude, then strutting his so-called manhood down the hall to his room. The response from my friend was not equal to everyones expectations. I'm sure they thought that he would stare at this young man and then probably say some sort of lewd comment. Instead my friend turned his head and walked into my cell to avoid the spectators view. By doing so he killed their party. My reaction was to become angry. I was going to approach these people and let them know what kind of ass---- they truly were. Instead I looked after my friend. He took the situation with a grain of salt and this was not the attitude I expected of him. Then he explained that this was just part of the territory of being gay. I've learned a valuable lesson from him. He is comfortable with who he is and his place in life. He has taken down those very walls which bound his tormentors, letting his true self shine through. He is loving, understanding, caring, and compassionate. In him I see where I most want to be in my emotional outlook on life.

We give situations the meaning they have for us. Theo's friend could have gotten furious, started yelling or fighting, and played into the scene. But because of his deeper understanding he didn't get pulled on stage.

> AS YOU GO THROUGH YOUR DAY CONSIDER:
> *I give situations the meaning they have for me,*
> *And I can choose the way I relate to them.*
> *The power of decision is my own.*

PAUSE AND REVIEW

Remember that your perceptions are a choice. How you see people and circumstances has a great deal to do with the way you'll feel. If you are living in the crowded conditions that are common to so many prisons and jails, every day you are likely to come in contact with people who have a lot of emotional problems. They may look like they are twenty or forty years old on the outside, but because they've never healed from childhood neglect and abuse, they may be emotionally frozen as a seven-year-old on the inside. You can get mad at someone for acting out like a hurting seven-year-old or a very insecure eleven-year-old who is trying to get approval from his or her "friends" in whatever way is possible . Or, you can see that person's Self and the part who is a hurting seven-year-old or an insecure eleven-year-old. And, as a result of seeing the bigger picture, choose not to get hooked in. Rather than hooking in to the fear and the crazy behavior that is often a product of being deeply troubled, remember that there is another way of looking at what's going on. If you do get pulled in emotionally, remember to be gentle with yourself. If you are human you will get pulled in from time to time.

WHEN YOU FEEL STRESSED CONSIDER:
There is another way of looking at the world.
AND   *I could choose peace instead of this.*

Being a Victim vs. Having a Victim Mentality

You may be the victim of certain people and circumstances, but you do not have to go through your day or life with a victim mentality.

I recently saw an interview on TV. with a man who had done fifteen years of a life sentence. After fifteen years his innocence was determined, and he was released from prison. He is now employed as a street social worker in Boston. The woman who interviewed him asked if he was bitter about spending fifteen years of his life in prison for a crime he didn't commit. He responded that he didn't have time to be bitter. He said that life was too short to waste on bitterness, that he wanted to put his energy into living in the present in a positive way. This man is a powerful example of someone who was a victim but was choosing not to go through life with a victim mentality. A victim mentality would unquestionably leave him bitter, angry, and miserable every day of his life. He was choosing to have it be different.

Of course this man had been angry and had fought to be released from prison. Anger, when wisely channeled, can be powerful fuel for getting things done. When confronted with injustice, one way of empowering yourself is to work towards change, towards righting the wrong, towards real justice. Do what you can do. Once you have done what you are willing to do and can do to change things on an outer level, the rest of the work you have to do is internal.

AS YOU GO THROUGH YOUR DAY
CONSIDER THE FOLLOWING:

I give people and circumstances
the meaning they have for me.

Richard   Today was a fairly peaceful day. A few times I was almost triggered but thanks to a growing awareness, the trigger was never pulled. It is so much easier being at peace than being angry. Anger is far too draining and I know now that peace is possible for more of the time.

CHAPTER 9

Relaxation: Making Space for New Possibilities

ONE THING IS for sure, the nature of life is such that whoever we are, we will be confronted with various stresses. Prison has its own set of stresses, not the least of which is always having to live close to people you might rather not be around. For some prisoners who are getting out soon, the greatest stress may be the anticipation of making a successful go at a drug-free, honest, harmless, financially workable life on the outside.

Stress can make you feel even more cornered, more boxed-in than you actually are. When we're stressed we constrict physically, emotionally, and mentally. A stressed body feels uptight and unwell. Our breathing constricts, our muscles constrict, which often leads to a lot of aches and pains. Our range of feelings constrict. We're much more likely to find ourselves feeling anxious, overwhelmed, and angry. We mentally close around familiar ways of dealing with situations even if it's clear that our approach doesn't work. We keep obsessing on the same stressful thoughts over and over. Our mind becomes like a broken record playing the solutions (or non-solutions) that we've heard ourselves say so many times before. When we relax deeply, or let-go as in meditation, it's like we take the needle off the record. It then becomes possible to hear a new song and a deeper wisdom directing us toward greater options for dealing with our situation, as well as toward greater physical health and peace.

No one can always control their spontaneous reactions to life's stresses, but by learning how to relax, you can begin to "let-go" — to release tension in your body, and to loosen your hold to self-destructive thoughts, feelings, and cravings. Learning to relax truly makes space in your life for new possibilities. It puts you in touch with greater ease and peace. It then opens the way to new possibilities and choices. As you relax and your stress lessens, even if you remain in the same cell, you are less likely to feel "boxed-in" or trapped.

If you practice relaxation on a regular basis you will be better prepared for the countless stressful curve balls that life throws your way. Even in the midst of unexpected challenges, it becomes easier to shift gears — and move from a stressed-out state to a calmer and wiser state of being.

Before we look at "how to" relax, take a few minutes to do a personal inventory. The signs of being stressed vary from person to person. If you've lived with a great deal of stress for years you may have become so used to the symptoms of stress that you don't even notice them now. Check off which of these signs of stress you frequently experience.

....

PAUSE AND REFLECT

Physical:
☐ difficulty breathing   ☐ headaches   ☐ fatique   ☐ insomnia
☐ weight change   ☐ muscle tension   ☐ pounding heart
☐ teeth grinding   ☐ foot-tapping or finger-drumming
☐ increased cigarette smoking
☐ heavy use of drugs, alcohol, or any addiction

☐ restlessness ☐ ulcers ☐ digestive problems
☐ frequent colds and flu

Emotional:

☐ anxiety ☐ depression ☐ easily discouraged
☐ usually frustrated ☐ mood swings ☐ bad temper
☐ nightmares ☐ unmotivated ☐ worry a lot
☐ angry much of the time

Mental:

☐ negative attitude ☐ complaining most of the time
☐ confusion ☐ boredom ☐ preoccupation
☐ negative self-talk (putting yourself down) ☐ forgetfulness
☐ little willingness to co-operate with others

Spiritual:

☐ feel empty ☐ life seems to have no meaning ☐ cynical
☐ unforgiving ☐ looking for magic

Relational:

☐ isolation ☐ distrust (of everyone) ☐ using people
☐ no willingness to establish friendships ☐ intolerance
☐ hostile and resentful

In this and the next chapter you will be introduced to two basic techniques for reducing stress — relaxation and meditation. Actually, describing these techniques as ways to "reduce stress" is only a small part of what they do; in addition they are powerful tools for building a strong foundation for physical, emotional and spiritual health and well-being.

Relax

Relaxation helps our bodies to release muscular tension, as well as bring our entire body chemistry into greater balance. Relaxation exercises can function like release valves on a radiator. Have you ever "blown up" at people? Have you ever felt so much pressure inside that there seemed to be no choice but to explode? Relaxation exercises (as well as the other approaches that are taught here) can help to relieve the pressure so that you don't get to the point when you feel like blowing up. (Many people find physical exercise a great release as well. Even though it isn't addressed in this book, I strongly encourage you to do some regular physical exercise.)

Relaxation techniques can help you open up to new ways of dealing with stressful issues. But like everything else that is taught in this book, relaxation must be put into practice to have an effect. An important thing to remember, however, is that a little regular practice can go a long way.

Relax. The word itself might conjure up visions of a beach, fishing, vacations, having a drink, smoking a joint. Though the ideas about the best time, place, and ways to relax vary from person to person, most of us have a pretty specific idea of what situations are most (and least) relaxing for us. Usually these ideas tie in with where we are, what we're doing, and what we feel has worked for us in the past. We can relax at home but not in a prison; we can relax if we're reading a book but not at a job; we can relax if we're stoned but not if we're straight.

Certainly it's not possible to leave prison to head for the beach. If you work, it may not be possible to leave your job to read a good book. And, in truth, getting stoned does much more to numb you out than to get you genuinely relaxed.

Relaxing in prison may seem impossible at first. And the thought of letting go into deep relaxation may feel threatening, like you won't have your defenses up in case of an attack. However, if it is safe enough for you to go to sleep, it is safe enough to relax. And, of course, you will want to choose a time and place that feels best for you.

With practice you can learn to be more relaxed most anytime. Relaxation may mean just taking a few moments now and then to let go of worries and concerns in order to return to whatever you're doing feeling more centered and energized. Think of the power and strength of a black belt in karate or any other accomplished martial artist. Their power isn't generated from their fear or muscle mass, it is generated from their skill and centerdness.

At first, learning to relax often requires the specific practice of some relaxation techniques. *Ultimately though, relaxation is not so much a technique as it is an attitude that allows you to remain more calm and clear even in the midst of upset and confusion.* And far from being "laid back," when you're truly relaxed you're likely to feel more alert and alive, as well as more comfortable with yourself and the world around you.

Relaxation Techniques

BREATHING

Whenever you're stressed, your breathing tends to become rapid and shallow. Noticing your breathing pattern and intentionally changing it is one of the simplest yet most important stress-reducing skills one can learn. By simply breathing deeply and evenly, breathing slows down, tense muscles relax, and you can quiet a worrying mind.

The following are some simple breathing exercises. Take some time everyday for the next week to give them a try. Your mind will naturally wander from time to time as you do these. Once you notice your mind wandering, without judging yourself, gently let go and return to wherever you left off. Also never judge your level of relaxation. Just pat yourself on the back and appreciate yourself for doing it.

• As you go through your day remind yourself to BREEEEEEATHE. Remember to breathe fully and deeply. In general, the deeper you are breathing, the more relaxed you will be.

- Breathe in to the count of 4- Breathe out to the count of 4. Breathe in to the count of 4, out to 4. Then (at the same speed) breathe in to 4 and out to 8. Then breathe in to 4, and out to 8. Then breathe in to the count of 4, and out to the count of 12. And in to 4, and out to 12.

Then, stop counting and just enjoy the fullness of your breathing.

- Deep Belly Breathing: Pay attention to your breathing.

Breathe in deeply through your nose, letting your stomach muscles expand as far as they can. Exhale through your mouth, letting your stomach muscles contract. Let out a sigh as you exhale. Feel your facial muscles, shoulders, and the rest of your body relax as you exhale. Repeat several times.

SELF-SUGGESTION AND BREATHING

- Repeat a word or phrase that makes a self-suggestion for relaxing and letting-go of tension. For example:

Inhale, and as you inhale, say to yourself: "*I am...*" Exhale, and as you exhale, say to yourself "*...relaxed.*" As you continue to repeat these words in rhythm with your breathing, let your breathing become a little deeper and a little slower. Try this for three or four minutes. If you notice your mind wondering, gently escort it back to your self-suggestion.

Some other self suggestions are :
With each in breath, "I breathe in a calm and soothing energy ... with each out breath, "I am releasing tension and worries."
Breathe in, "I give myself permission," breathe out "to relax now."

BODY SCAN AND BREATHING

- Scan your body. Notice how different parts of you are feeling. As you inhale, imagine you are breathing clear, soothing, healing energy into areas that feel tired, painful, or tight. As you exhale, imagine the tiredness, the pain, and/or the tightness leaving with the out breath.

Scan your entire body from your toes to your head. Breathe in a soothing, calming energy with each inhalation. Breathe out tension with each exhalation. Go from one body part to the next. Start with your feet. Put all your attention on your feet. Imagine breathing in a soothing, calming energy, as if you were breathing in air directly from a beautiful, peaceful place in nature. Then breathe out and feel that part of your body relaxing. Feel the muscles relax.

Then one at a time, do the same with your ankles, lower legs, knees, thighs, the lower part of the trunk of your body, your stomach, lower back, along your spine, chest, upper back, shoulders, arms, hands, fingers, neck, jaw muscles, face, forehead, scalp.

Then bring your awareness to your entire body and breathe in the peaceful energy into your entire body for a while longer.

POSITIVE VISUALIZATION

Images in your mind have an immediate and profound effect on your physical and emotional state. Have you ever woken from a frightening dream and found your heart racing, your muscles seized in tension, and perhaps even noticed that you were sweating or shaking, all while you were in a perfectly safe place? This is a clear example of how images in your mind effect you. Here you were in a safe place and because of the images in your dream, your mind and body reacted as if the incident were actually happening. Your nervous system can't tell the difference between something that is actually occuring and something that is happening purely in your imagination. In the same way, if you imagine relaxing and peaceful experiences, your nervous system doesn't know that you're not actually lying on that beach in the Carribean or walking through a beautiful park. When you visualize yourself feeling relaxed and confident, you are programming yourself for physical health, success, and feeling good.

- Peaceful Scene: Take a few deep relaxing breaths, then using as many senses (ie. seeing, hearing, smelling) as possible, imagine yourself in your most ideal environment for relaxation. Give yourself the gift of this mini-vacation often.

- Daily Life Scene: Take a few deep relaxing breaths, then using as many senses as possible, imagine yourself calm, clear, and confident moving through your day. Imagine yourself feeling this way in a potentially stressful situation.

HOLY MOMENT

The Holy or Whole Moment exercise is a powerful relaxation created by Dr. Joan Borysenko, teacher and author of *Guilt is the Teacher, Love is the Lesson* and *Fire in the Soul*. A holy or whole moment, refers to a moment in which we feel whole and complete. In other words when we aren't thinking "if only' I had this or "if only" I had that or if only I were somewhere else — then I would feel really good and be okay. It is a moment when we feel peaceful and whole, when nothing else is needed to feel this way.

Toward the end of this exercise there is what is referred to as a grounding or anchoring technique. This technique has been proven to help store the memory of the wholeness or relaxation in your body (or nervous system) so that when you want to tap into the peaceful feelings at times when it isn't possible to go through the entire exercise, you can simply put your fingers together and your body will immediately recall and recreate the feelings of calm.

Take about five minutes now to do this exercise. Read each step. Do it for a minute, then go on to the next.

- Recall a time in your life when the past and future slipped away and you were totally present, at peace, open to the fullness of the moment — perhaps a time while in nature, or while enjoying a special sunset or sunrise. (If you can't recall one, create one in your imagination now.)

Recall what this experience was like. How did it feel?

Where did you experience the peace and fullness of the moment in your body?

Breathe and fully recall the experience.

Then gently ground or anchor the experience by gently touching the thumb and the finger next to the thumb together. If you are right-handed, do this with your right hand. If you are left-handed, do this with your left hand.

As you go through your day remember to return to the feelings of this holy or whole moment by touching your fingers together. Breathe and give yourself permission to enjoy the full and peaceful feelings of this "holy moment."

Tom Today I had an experience where in the past I would have felt totally justified in becoming angry. It all started when I went outside in the yard. Some guys were playing catch with a softball. So I grabbed a glove and joined the game. We were pitching back and forth enjoying ourselves. For the first time in a long time I started to relax and of all places to relax a prison is one of the hardest. Well the good time soon ended when a wild throw came toward me. It was about five feet over my head but I still tryed to catch it. Needless to say I missed. The ball landed in a pack of officers. No one was hurt and I presumed all was well. So I go to retrieve the ball and I was smiling. Well the cop holding the ball didn't see a need for me to smile. He says, "So you think that's funny." I told him that I didn't and he persisted in being a _____. He then told me to put my glove away and take a walk. Now I was becoming angry and where I really wanted to put that glove wasn't back in the bag. Then I remembered something I had told myself after the second class: "Tom, you're not the same person this week that you were last week." Before my thoughts could get much further than they were I felt my forefinger touch my thumb. So I went with the feeling. I caught my breath and began to breath out the negative energy from the incident with me and the cop and I started taking in the positive energy of the feelings and thoughts that are in the Holy place. Then after calming down I tried to think of where his anger was coming from and why it was directed at me. The bottom line was safety. His safety and that of the officers around him. I didn't agree with his way of handling the situation, but I did see where he was coming from. After going through all this in my mind I became happy with myself and the situation that presented itself. It gave me a chance to try the methods out and it worked better than I would have imagined.

In a way there's certainly nothing new about the things I've described in this chapter. Clearly you are breathing all the time. Two minutes without a breath and life, as you know it, is over. It's not really that you need to remember to breathe. You'll breathe whether you remember to or not. It's that you need to remember to breathe a little more deeply from time to time so that your brain can be nourished with the oxygen that it needs to be alert and so your body can relax and release the tension that keeps it locked up.

And just as surely as we breathe, we are giving ourselves "self-suggestions" all the time; "I can't do it." "I'm not good enough." "I can't relax here." Sometimes it's simply a matter of which suggestion we choose and buy into that brings us to a dead end or to greater possibility.

In the same way, we are visualizing all the time. We may see ourselves in a confrontation with someone a thousand times before it happens. We can also begin to use our imagination creatively, seeing ourselves in potentially stressful situations being relaxed and responding in wise and constructive ways. Which ever way we see it, life is much more likely to play itself out that way.

And if there's any place most people don't consider holy ground, it's prison. But holy ground is any ground where you let go of tension and open to the peace and fullness of the moment. In a holy moment there are no boundaries. If only for a moment we escape the limits of a tense and closed mind and feel a connection to the limitless peace of the Self.

FROM TIME TO TIME REMEMBER TO BREEEEEEATHE,
AND CONSIDER THE POSSIBILITY THAT:

Within me is a peacefulness
that cannot be disturbed.

CHAPTER 10

Awareness and Meditation: Getting Clear on What's Really Going On

THE WORD "MEDITATION" may bring images to mind of a man with a beard and turban sitting cross-legged on a mountain top. Even though meditation has its roots in the ancient past, its powerful potential for reducing stress and promoting inner peace has made it the backbone of every highly successful stress-reduction program that I know of. In all the courses that I teach, whether in prisons, businesses, or medical settings, I give the instruction and practice of meditation a great deal of time and attention. My enthusiasm comes not only from its positive impact on my own life, but from seeing over and over how valuable meditation is for anyone who is willing to do it.

Wilma I am starting to understand myself better now that I have been able to put the time into meditating. The days that I do it, I'm a more peaceful person. I find that I feel much better afterward, more clear minded, relaxed and ready to approach the day with a better attitude. I feel meditation is like a switch, allowing me the choice between past and present.

Mike The meditation is something I never would have considered before but now I'm going to practice it on a regular basis. I definitely feel more at peace with myself and I seem to deal with pressure much better. I didn't meditate for a few weeks and then I started meditating in my cell again. It was like getting together with a good friend I hadn't seen for a while.

Pat I'm a lot more relaxed. I'm now able to sit with pain, fear and anxiety until it passes. It helps me with my headaches and it has helped me with coping with the holidays and missing my family.

Dick I have learned that meditation is a very useful tool in coming to a place where I can take an honest look at myself and straighten out the problems that have been suppressed deep within for such a long time. Meditation gives me a chance to listen to myself. Like a compass, it puts me on course.

Awareness Meditation

If someone told you they danced, you wouldn't know if they were talking about swing, hip-hop, ballet, salsa, waltzing, or any other of a thousand forms of dance. What you might assume is that they listen to music and move their body in a certain way to a particular rhythm. In the same way, if someone told you that they meditated, you wouldn't know if they contemplated a certain thought, focused their eyes on an image, repeated a word or sound in their mind, focused their attention on their breathing, or any other of a hundred forms of meditation. What you might assume is that they quiet their mind and focus their attention. Meditation has many forms but central to all of them is focusing one's attention and awareness.

The form of meditation I teach in this chapter is called "awareness", "insight" or "mindfulness" meditation. This form of meditation is the foundation of many highly respected stress reduction programs offered in hospitals and medical centers around the country. Medical centers often teach meditation because of its physical benefits. But as one often quickly discovers meditation has many psychological and spiritual benefits as well. Meditation has nothing to do with a religious belief system. If you are devoted to a particular religion, my guess is that by meditating you will connect even more deeply to it.

Over the years I've learned many forms of meditation but I've come back to "awareness meditation" as the one I prefer to practice. All forms of meditation have value, and I don't know that any one way of meditating is better than another. But I teach this way because I have found it most useful in cultivating balance, awareness, and insight — factors that are all necessary for being truly free.

Living with Greater Awareness

Consider a typical day: It may begin with the thought "I should get up" and is certain to be followed by a succession of other thoughts. "Where are my pants? What time is it? I'm hungry. I have to pee. I forgot to send that letter yesterday. I have to get that letter out today. My back aches. Another day in this hole. It's hopeless. I wonder if I'll get a letter today. I love her. I hope they ship that guy out. Is it only Tuesday? I wonder if I'll get a visit. I have to remember to send that form." And on and on, an endless stream of thoughts and feelings running through the mind. Each takes its turn taking up our attention throughout the day until we go to sleep.

Most of us identify with the thoughts, feelings, and body sensations that are most intense at any given moment, even though they are only a small part of who we are. The Self, the part of us that is aware, can stand back and observe all these changing thoughts, feelings, and sensations. With awareness you can have thoughts without being controlled by any one of them. You can have feelings without being overwhelmed or run by them. You can have strong sensations without being consumed by them. When you're stressed, you are identifying with your thoughts and feelings. It's as if your head is in a cloud and you can't see the calm, clear sky which, like awareness, is always there.

Sometimes when we first start to meditate we see how active the mind is. We see all the thoughts and feelings and think that our mind is getting noisier or more agitated than ever before. Actually this is just an indication that we are becoming quieter. We become aware of just how noisy and demanding our thoughts and feelings have always been.

By meditating you develop the ability to step back and quiet the mind. You become the observer of your experience as well as a participant. You slow down long enough to see the play of the mind. You learn to separate the part of your mind that is almost always busy thinking, planning, judging, remembering, fantasizing and ruminating from your calm, clear, quiet mind which is just awareness itself.

The meditation helps you to find some stillness in the very center of your thoughts and emotional states. When you discover this stillness in meditation, you are increasingly able to be in the middle of a dorm room or a commotion and still find some balance and inner stability.

I've known a number of men who regularly got disciplinary reports and were locked down time and time again. After they started meditating they found this pattern totally change. They didn't "try" not to fight or get pulled into the drama around them, they were just more aware and as a result they didn't feel drawn to react as they did before.

As you meditate or "practice awareness" instead of acting on all your thoughts, you become increasing able to choose which ones you really want to act on. Instead of being an actor at the mercy of your emotions, you become both the uncritical observer and the skilled director of your life.

The "Right" Attitude for Meditation

Author and meditation teacher Jon Kabat-Zinn sums it up well in his book, *Full Catastrophe Living*, when he writes about the attitudes we can bring to the practice of meditation. He says we can bring one of the following:

(1) Meditation won't work for me, in which case everything you experience will build up a case for this.

(2) Meditation will change my life overnight. Here your expectations are so great that you will get discouraged quickly and abandon it.

(3) You are open to the meditation but skeptical. This is the best attitude. Here you're saying you don't know if it will be helpful for you; you may have your doubts about it's value if you have never meditated before, but you're willing to try it and be open to what it brings.

The famous American auto maker, Henry Ford, once said, "Those who believe they can do something and those who believe they can't, are both right." If you believe you can't meditate, you will prove yourself right. If you believe you can, you will also prove yourself right. *It's really a matter of willingness.*

EXERCISE

How to Meditate

1. Find a comfortable sitting position where your back is straight, but not rigid and your body is balanced and at ease. Place your hands comfortably in your lap or on your knees. Close your eyes if you are comfortable doing so. If you aren't comfortable closing your eyes, you can choose a place nearby and focus your vision in a relaxed way.

2. Bring your attention to your breathing. At first you can focus on the belly rising and falling. Just feel your breath. Notice the chang-

ing sensations in your body as you breathe in and out. Don't try to control your breathing in any way. Breathe naturally. Sometimes your breathing may be deep; sometimes it may be shallow. Your "job" is to simply be aware of the breath, feeling the changing sensations of the entire rising movement and the entire falling movement.

3. Your mind will naturally wander from its focus on your breathing. As soon as you become aware that it is wandering, simply notice what your mind has wandered to. And then gently let go of your thoughts. Let go of the past and the future, and return your awareness to your breathing.

4. After focusing on the belly for a while, you can expand your awareness of the movement of the breath beyond the belly area.

Become aware of the changing sensations of the breath throughout more of the body now.

5. Do this everyday. You are strongly encouraged to take fifteen or twenty minutes at least once a day. If possible, choose a regular time.

6. After you have meditated for a week or so, if you wish you can expand the meditation further. When you notice that your attention has wandered from the breath, you can either simply notice that it has wandered, gently let go and bring your attention back to the breath as you have been doing. Or, you can make a mental note of what your mind has wandered to. Give it a name — labeling it in general as "thinking", "feeling", "sensing" "hearing."

Or, you can be more specific and label it as "anger", "fear", "judging", "planning," "sadness," "happiness," "desire," "impatience", "sound" or whatever. Without analyzing your thoughts and feelings — without hanging on to them or pushing them away — see them as they are. Simply observe them without judging them. Then anchor your awareness in the breathing again.

* * *

INFORMAL MEDITATION, OR
MEDITATING THROUGHOUT THE DAY

In addition to the more formal meditation practice when you set a special time aside, you can practice informally throughout your day. Informal meditation can be done while walking, lifting weights, eating, exercising, looking into the sky, working — essentially any time throughout your day.

To meditate informally, become aware of your breathing from time to time during your day. Do this for a few breaths. Intentionally bring your full attention to the present moment. Become aware of whatever is happening. Notice any thoughts and feelings in these moments. Just be aware of them without judging them.

Common Questions and Comments About Meditation

The following are questions and comments about meditation that came out of the prison courses. They are the common issues that arise for most anyone.

- *Is it okay to lie down to meditate, rather than sitting up?*

During the "formal" practice of meditation *it is okay to lie down, but you are encouraged to sit up in a stable, grounded position with your back straight, while relaxed.* The sitting posture (whether your feet are on the floor or you are sitting on a pillow with your legs crossed) reinforces being awake and conscious, the mental states that you are trying to cultivate in the practice. The mind is naturally more likely to wonder and drift if you are lying down.

- *I'm trying, but it's hard to stay focused.*

It's probably impossible to stay focused for long periods of time. When you start meditating you realize very quickly that the mind has a mind of it's own. There is a saying, "You can't stop the mind from wandering any more that you can stop yourself from getting older." The wandering mind is just part of the process of meditation. Your attention will naturally move away from the breath many times. Within moments your mind may start to doubt, evaluate, or criticize. The important thing to understand is that noticing that the mind has wandered and then coming back to the breath again, without judging, *is* the practice of meditation.

When your mind wanders (once you become aware that it has wandered —whether it is a second later or five minutes later), greet it with an attitude of "No big deal." It's just the mind wandering. Then ease your attention back to the breath again. Come back to the present moment. As Father Thomas Keating writes in his book *Open Mind, Open Heart,* "Resist no thought, hang on to no thought, react emotionally to no thought. Whatever image, feeling, reflection or experience attracts your attention, return..." to the movement of the breath in your body.

Rather than thinking about staying focused for the next five minutes, it's much more realistic to think about staying focused just for the next breath. See if you can be aware from the beginning of the in-breath all the way to the end of the in-breath. Then be aware from the beginning of the out-breath, all the way to the end of the out-breath. Then be aware of the next in-breath. Feel the rising movement, then feel the falling movement. When your mind wanders, gently yet decisively bring your attention back to the breath again. Know that even if your mind wanders a hundred or a thousand times in an hour, the meditation still has great value. As you do this the mind becomes steadier and more balanced and stable.

Your job is not to judge how you are doing, your job is just to do it.

• *Sometimes I feel peaceful when I meditate, sometimes I feel agitated. Could I be doing it right?*

The practice of awareness meditation is simple but not easy. Before you know it, you may find yourself having a wide variety of experiences. You may feel peaceful and calm while meditating, or you may feel restless and agitated. Your mind may be quiet and still or turbulent with onrushing thoughts. You may find it easy to focus on your breathing or you may find it nearly impossible to do so for more than a few moments at a time. Whatever your experience of the awareness meditation is, it is correct and likely to change tomorrow.

As long as you follow the guidelines suggested, and give the practice your sincere commitment, you are doing the meditation correctly.

• *I let go of my thoughts, but I often find myself lost in them in what seems like a second later.*

Sometimes strong thoughts and feelings won't just go away because we return to the breath. Sometimes "letting go" of your thoughts and feelings means just "letting them be." Let your thoughts and feelings be in the background, while your primary attention is on the breathing.

It's like the image of clouds again. When you are lost in the thought or feeling it is like your head is in the cloud and you mistake the cloud for the entire sky. Once you notice yourself lost in restlessness (or whatever), you can pull your head down from the cloud. The cloud won't necessarily go away, the restlessness may not disappear. But now it is a cloud rather the the entire sky. It is part of your experience, rather than your entire experience. And like any state of mind, it will eventually pass.

As you meditate you tap into something deeper and greater in yourself, a part of your true nature that has been obscured by the mental clamoring of thoughts and emotions.

• *Sometimes its really difficult to meditate when I'm feeling angry or frustrated. It's hard to be there with myself. I'd rather get up and walk away.*

It's hard to be present to our own pain and misery. It can feel overwhelming, like that's all there is and that's all there will ever be.

It can be extremely difficult to sit with emotions that drugs or alcohol or whatever may have numbed out before. It takes courage. Appreciate yourself for being willing to sit with them!!

How can you work with these feelings in meditation? As meditation teacher Jack Kornfield simply and accurately put it, "when strong emotions arise one of three things will happen; (1) they'll go away, (2) they'll stay the same, or (3) they'll get worse. You're job isn't to control that. You're job is to find a kind of balance and openness with them."

As you meditate you develop a spacious mind. A spacious mind helps you to deal with life's sorrows in a deeply healing way. Think of putting a spoonful of nasty tasting salt in a small glass of water. Because of the size of the container, if you drink it, the water is going to taste bad. If, however, you put that spoonful of salt in a body of water the size of a bathtub or lake and then drink a glassful, it's obviously not going to have the same effect.

As meditation teacher Sharon Salzburg wrote, "Meditation is not about getting rid of the salt in our lives. It's about creating the spaciousness of mind with which we can meet all of life's experiences with peace and equanimity." It's not about escaping our feelings but rather allowing for the truth of our feelings while resting in the center of them. The power of meditation grows when we can sit not only with the increasing inner peace, but with our anger, sorrow, doubt, desires, anxiety — when we can sit with them and watch them as they arise and pass away rather than trying to run from them. As we do this, we give birth to a new kind of fearlessness and strength.

In meditation we begin to make the distinction between our thoughts and feelings and the mind's reaction to them. There is a great difference between being aware of emotions and being submerged in them. When we're submerged in them, they rapidly evoke other emotions. There is *more* annoyance, anger, self-pity, whatever. When we identify with our emotions we're apt to get lost in a drama of the imagination before we even know it has happened.

In meditation, we can begin to see the difference between thoughts and feelings that arise and what the mind does with them. When we can develop this spacious mind and be there for ourselves in this way, we begin to end the tyranny and oppression of our own negative thoughts and emotions. Personal freedom starts here.

We sit, open to whatever arises, not judging any of it, just watching without getting pulled in for long. When we do this over time, new mental states arise. Agitation, frustration, and restlessness transform into moments of increasing peace.

Walter I've begun meditating in the room when it is dark and everything quiets down. I feel the impulses to get away from meditating. They're very strong but my will seeks to know more of myself. I found that if I meditate it's a way of showing myself love. I enjoy it because it allows me to care for myself. It keeps me away from the senseless desires or intangible feelings of approval that I sought after in drugs and alcohol. It's a very decent way to feel.

● *Soon after I start meditating, I seem to fall asleep or get tired.*

As with anything else that arises during meditation, the most skillful way to initially deal with it, is simply to pay attention to it. What does sleepiness feel like in the body and mind? Sometimes naming it — sleepiness — and just paying close attention to the experience of sleepiness will wake you up and allow you to continue with the meditation. You can also meditate with your eyes open, or even standing up. Sometimes practical actions like throwing a little cold water on your face can help.

Sleepiness usually has three origins. One is that you are genuinely tired. Perhaps you haven't been sleeping well. At times like this what you might need most is just to go to sleep. Another kind of sleepiness comes upon us when we want to avoid something, when we don't want to remember or experience a fearful or unpleasant state. When we get sleepy and our body isn't actually tired, it is often a sign of resistance. At these moments Jack Kornfield, in his book *A Path With Heart,* encourages us to ask ourselves, "What is going on here, what am I avoiding by falling asleep?" He writes that, "Many times we will discover an important fear or difficulty just underneath it. States of loneliness, sorrow, emptiness, and loss of control of some aspect of our life are common ones that we fall asleep to avoid, When we recognize this, our whole practice can open up to a new level."

The third reason meditation sometimes leaves us feeling sleepy is that, if we are used to keeping very busy and running around most of the time, just calming down can unconsciously trigger the thought that it's time to go to sleep. If you notice this kind of sleepiness, name it, sit up, and bring your full attention back to the fullness of the moment, back to the breath. As Kornfield points out, "Underneath the sleepiness is the possibility of true peace and rest."

● *How can you meditate when there is so much noise around?*

The way to deal with noise while you're meditating is the same way as you deal with anything else that arises when you're meditating — without resisting it, judging it or getting caught up in it, just notice it. Simply notice "sound." Sounds just passing through the calm open space of the awareness. Don't label the sounds as "voice" or "banging" or "music" or whatever it happens to be. Just simply notice sound as sound. In the meditation, everything that arises is given equal attention and equal value. Rather than judging one sound as pleasant and another sound as unpleasant, from that place of pure awareness, you would simply notice sounds coming and going in your environment.

Richard I was very doubtful of it's effect in the beginning but now I use meditation as a way of becoming aware and as an observation tool. One example of this is I know how difficult it is to concentrate with all the commotion that goes on in the tiers, but this can work to your advantage. It can teach you to just be aware that sounds and noise are only that, sounds and noise. You can commit yourself to hearing all the sounds and distractions of prison, and still just become "aware" of them, choosing to acknowledge them as just that — sounds. I feel this teaches you how to deal with the many problems that occur during a prison stay. It allows you to see people in a different light. Your judgments become understanding. Your hates become tolerance. And your attitude becomes more open.

• *I keep finding excuses not to meditate. When I meditate I know I benefit from it, but its hard to find the time.*

I once heard a story of a man who had spent ten years in solitary confinement in a Chinese concentration camp prison. He had no contact with the outside world and he didn't know if he would ever be released. When he finally was released he appeared to be in an exceptionally good frame of mind considering what he had endured. People asked him how he was able to stay sane and emotionally together after being isolated for all that time. He attributed his state of mind to the fact that he had meditated every day. He said the meditation had helped him to make the most of each day and to stay in the present rather than being consumed with worry about the future. The thing about his story that most stood out for me was his statement that he had to work to find the time to meditate every day. Here he was in solitary confinement and still it was a challenge for him to not let other things distract him from meditating. And you can be sure he didn't have a T.V.

In truth, regardless of our schedule, whether we have endless hours with nothing to do or we are busy with many activities, we rarely *find* the time to meditate. We have to *create* it, or we're likely to find ourselves doing something else.

If you want to meditate, yet find that it is time to go to sleep and you haven't gotten to it, be gentle with yourself. Don't make yourself wrong, but know that each day is an opportunity to choose again. Actually, if it's the end of the day and you're too tired to sit for fifteen minutes, perhaps you can meditate for just a few minutes as a way of reinforcing your commitment to yourself. As one inmate put it, "We're not going to always feel like meditating but the important thing is to put some time into it. I've found that even one moment spent with Self has more value than none."

It's very helpful to meditate around the same time everyday so it becomes a regular part of your schedule. I find it most helpful to meditate in the morning because it sets a tone for the day. As one inmate wrote, "I find that I can start my day with an even mood. Problems still come up, but I seem to deal with all of them regardless. I feel much more relaxed now. I know it's from the meditation." Many inmates find that count is a good time to meditate.

As Joan Borysenko wrote in her book *Fire in The Soul*, "By meditating instead of identifying our life with the succession of boats (thoughts) that go down the river, we begin to identify it as the river. As we do so, the reality that the boats are merely passing by but the river is ever-present comes into focus, and our perception about what is real and what is unreal shifts." Later she writes "My all-time favorite meditation is a small, moist piece of chocolate cake eaten with exquisite attention and tremendous gratitude. Any time that we are fully present in the moment, we are meditating. We are free from the limitations of thought and at one with the river of life."

If we aren't present we overlook the possibilities for growth and transformation that exist in each moment. We miss so many possibilities. Imagine if we were really present and awake to our lives. How many more colors would we see at sunset? How much more exhilarating might exercise feel? How many more positive choices would we make? How many more of our deepest instincts would we follow? How much more understanding would we have for ourselves and for others? How many more moments of peace might we experience?

Meditation is not about looking for a special experience. It is about being present to the fullness of the moment. It is about seeing what is really going on.

I can be the observer of my experience as well as a participant

PART 4

CHAPTER 11

Restoring Dignity: Facing Guilt, Shame, and the Impact of Crime

Reggie I can understand anyones reasoning when they try to hide or repress accepting their past. But I now realize it is not the way to go. The pain, guilt, shame and remorse will only come back at every opportunity. Most of us know deep in our hearts that we have wronged someone else, especially loved ones. But knowing it and really acknowledging it are two different feelings altogether. I refuse to hide from my self any longer. I know my own heart and I'm not the inconsiderate, miserable, uncaring man I have forced my self to be.

FACING ONE'S GUILT, shame, and the actual impact of abuse and crime on one's victims can be extremely difficult and painful. But confronting these issues is a necessary prerequisite for any real healing and self-forgiveness. Without coming to terms with these issues, dignity cannot be restored and self-forgiveness can never be achieved.

Many inmates feel tremendous guilt and remorse for the choices they have made and the pain they have caused. Many are consumed by guilt, remorse, and shame — so much so that it turns on them, keeping them in a closed cycle of low self-esteem and destructive choices. At the opposite end of the spectrum are those individuals who have caused pain and acted with no integrity, yet have rarely, if ever, felt guilt or remorse for their actions. A few people may actually have nothing to feel guilty about, but I suspect that most people who feel no guilt aren't being totally honest with themselves.

The prison environment can act to undermine this honesty. As one inmate who is in for murder said, "It is hard to feel remorse in an environment that is so brutal. I didn't feel sorry and remorseful for what I had done for about three years after coming to prison because I was too busy trying to survive. I was focusing on taking care of me. Even if a part of you is willing to look at it, you feel like it's not a safe enough place."

Many people feel guilty but are not consciously aware of their guilt. Drugs and alcohol are often used to keep the uneasy and sometimes agonizing feelings of guilt at a distance. One inmate put his experience this way, "Once I quit drugs and reflected back, then I realized how much pain I was causing. You don't feel guilty until you straighten up. I was so full of my own pain, I didn't want to look at myself." Many people are in denial, refusing to take responsibility when it is theirs, spending a great deal of energy justifying their actions, and projecting their guilt onto others as anger and blame.

Until we are honest with ourselves about what we have done — whether it was terribly abusive or just mildly hurtful — the guilt feelings which arise from these actions control us at some unconscious level and keep us from healing. Cleaning up begins by telling the truth. We often avoid self honesty out of a desire to avoid the unpleasantness of the truth. Yet in order to heal we have to develop a genuine compassion for ourselves while, at the same time, enduring a ruthless honesty about our own experiences of darkness.

Guilt

When I write about guilt I am not referring to legal guilt but to one's personal experience of guilt.

Healthy guilt is a feeling that arises when we believe we have done something wrong or immoral. It is a matter of responding to our own highest sense of integrity. It relates to behaviors or thoughts that we don't condone, that don't reflect our deepest sense of what is respectful, honest, and just. If we are raised in a reasonably loving and respectful home and are basically healthy, an appropriate sense of guilt develops at about three years old. Our experience of guilt posts boundaries indicating that our behavior and motivation are appropriate or inappropriate, caring or insensitive, have integrity or lack integrity. Healthy guilt guides our conscience.

A Lack of Empathy and the Seeds of Evil

As mentioned earlier, when children are hurt, rejected, and deprived, the numbing of their feelings is a natural reaction. It can be their only protection against suffering. Because abuse and neglect often happen over and over in childhood, numbness becomes second nature and is maintained long after the threatening situation has changed. The numbness towards one's own pain then becomes numbness towards the pain of others as well. The numbness can manifest as passive indifference to the suffering of others' or, in its extreme, it becomes active cruelty. In some instances in order to make unbearable suffering more bearable, there is an unintentional and unconscious connection made in the child between pain, humiliation, and suffering — and pleasure. This connection is at the center of masochistic and sadistic fantasies and behavior.

It is this numbness to one's own pain that is at the core of much of what is considered evil.

The pain may lie hidden under years and layers of numbness; You may have *had* to become indifferent to your pain in order to survive. If this was the case, in order to heal, you must gently and with great compassion now peal away the layers of numbness and indifference to yourself. If, with help, each person took this task upon him or herself, I am confident that the existence of most cruelty, indifference, and evil would eventually be dispelled.

When Guilt Is Absent

There are people who have little or no internalized moral code, people who have not developed or are totally disconnected from a healthy sense of guilt and shame. In its extreme, people who lack any sense of guilt are known as sociopaths or psychopaths. They may commit what are referred to as "crimes without conscience," brutal acts of violence for which they have no feelings of guilt or remorse.

This extreme lack of conscience can be the result of many factors. It most often has its roots in severe childhood neglect and abuse and/or severe chemical imbalance or abuse. Acts that demonstrate this lack of conscience have been committed by children as young as five or six years old. A common trait of many "children without conscience" is a complete lack of physical and emotional bonding with a parent or caretaker in critical stages of early development. This lack of conscience is sometimes seen in children and adults who are the victims of "fetal alcohol syndrome," an impairment to the central nervous system caused by alcohol abuse by the mother during pregnancy. It often results in, among other traits, impaired ability to learn (it is the leading cause of mental retardation in the U.S.), poor communication skills, poor judgment, and impulsive behavior.

A Distorted Sense of Guilt

Some people's less extreme, but nonetheless, thwarted development of guilt may not be the result of severe trauma and abuse but rather the consequence of the numbing that results from learned behavior and low self-esteem. Feelings of unworthiness can result in a preoccupation with one's own needs and a lack of empathy for others. The absense of guilt can also be the result of what is learned in one's home, community, and culture. Tyrone's experience is an example of this.

Tyrone The message that I received from my parent was mostly that of "You're just gonna have to deal with it, life is never fair." That was pretty much the trend in my house. "Life will never be fair." I was taught to live by this. From there my life revolved around that way of thinking — the way I acted, the way I walked, the way I talked, my total being as a person became unfair. I figured by me being unfair to other people and to myself, it would come out to be fair in the long run. That in turn has made me think in all honesty, that the choices that I've made in life and mostly throughout my adult life, were good and in my best interest. Only the people who tried to be fair were the ones who failed. That was the way I believed life to be.

What Tyrone learned at home allowed him to rationalize any "unfair" or destructive behavior. With support he was able to step back and become aware of what he had learned and how this had influenced his choices. With his "un-numbing" and "un-learning" came a natural desire and willingness to show up as a more caring and responsible person.

All children first learn the difference between right and wrong at home. When adult role models are irresponsible and lacking in integrity, children learn to imitate their behavior.

PAUSE AND REFLECT

What did your parents (and other important role-models) teach you (by their attitudes and personal example) about respecting themselves and others?

What did you learn from your peers and other people in your community about respecting yourself and others?

If you watched your father beating your mother you might have mistakenly learned that beating women is acceptable behavior. If your mother beat you or your siblings, you may have mistakenly learned that beating children is nothing to feel guilty about. If people in your neighborhood used intimidation and violence to "settle" arguments, unless other ways to resolve conflicts were modeled in your home or encouraged elsewhere, you may feel (or have felt) justified in using violence. If you learned to hold deep prejudice and hate people, then you aren't likely to feel guilty if you hurt them. If you learn to view your world through a seriously distorted lens, you come to believe that reactions that are abusive, hurtful, and violent are reasonable and acceptable.

These learned behaviors and attitudes lead to a distorted perception of the world that thwarts and numbs a healthy sense of guilt. From the vantage point of these distorted perceptions, the ego can find a way to rationalize, blame, or justify almost anything. Abusive or violent behavior and/or crime are rationalized as "not being that serious." Or the victim "deserved" it. Or "everyone is doing it." Or, "if I don't do it, somebody else will." Or "They provoked me to the point where I had no choice" — which is rarely the case. All these rationalizations are just that — rationalizations. They are all created to protect one's self from looking at and coming to terms with the truth.

> **Bob** I've had to face all the hidden lies and deceit that I've been living with throughout my life. In the past I never accepted what I did as wrong and immoral and thus I ended up where I am. However, since re-examining myself I find that I am totally accountable for my actions and accept the responsibilities of my actions. It wasn't until I fully accepted what I did that healing could actually begin.

Sometimes it's incredibly difficult to face the truth. Perhaps you committed a crime that is at odds with how you see yourself. Perhaps you wonder, "How could I have done that?" or "What was I thinking?" Maybe it was a crime of passion or an act committed in a fit of rage or while stoned or drunk. It's hard to reconcile the behavior if you know in your heart it isn't the way you would have acted if you were thinking clearly. Yet, if one is guilty, in order to move on with inner freedom, the guilt has to be acknowledged and felt. Any denial or rationalization obscures the truth and stops one from taking the responsibility that must be taken in order to make the most of life now.

As Howard Zehr, author of *Changing Lenses: A New Focus on Crime and Justice* writes, "New life requires both forgiveness and confession. For offenders to be truly whole, they must confess wrongdoing, admitting their responsibility and acknowledging the harm done. Only then is it possible to repent, to turn one's life around and begin in a new direction."

The Impact of Crime and Abuse

Real honesty is not selective. It sees it all. *We have to shine a light on the entire truth — not in order to beat ourselves up, but in order to claim responsibility when it is ours.* Then we can learn from our past and move on to experience the emotional freedom that only the truth can give rise to. Then we can shift from denial and weakness to strength of character. From fear and ignorance to true dignity.

In crimes where there are victims, facing the full impact of our actions is a necessary part of healing. Being the victim of abuse and violence is often emotionally devastating for victims and, in the case of murder, for the victim's family and friends. Injury done to one person may be deeply wounding to an entire community. Even though it may be difficult, there is no way to be fully responsible or accountable for what we have done unless we start by naming it and telling the truth about it.

Unfortunately, very unfortunately, the existing legal system considers the state or federal government the victim of crime. For this reason, offenders who have committed crimes against individuals rarely get to see any of the effect that their actions have had on the real victims and their families.

In the period after a crime, most victims are overwhelmed with feelings of confusion, helplessness, terror, and vulnerability. These feelings are usually followed with feelings of anger, guilt, suspicion, depression, meaninglessness, self-doubt, and regret. There are the questions that may linger and haunt a person for a lifetime: Why me? Is the offender coming back? Did they have something personal against me? What could I have done to stop it from happening? As with all victims, there are feelings of shame and self-blame. The feelings may dominate for long periods of time and the effects may be far-reaching — affecting not only the victim's inner emotional life but also their relationship with their children, partner, family, and friends. Their ability to work may be affected, their ability to trust anyone, to have faith in a God they may feel has failed them can make their lives empty, painful, and meaningless for a long time. The act of a crime may be over, yet the victims carry the burden of fear, anger, and anguish.

Rob's experience is a clear and powerful example of the potentially devastating effects of being victimized.

Rob — A Victim's Account The last thing that would ever go through my mind that night was that I would be raped. Men don't get attacked that way!

I really thought he was my friend when he invited me to his apartment across the hall for a beer. When I joined him and his long-time partner, I was glad for the company. I hadn't lived very long in Washington and spent a lot of time by myself. After class, I'd usually go home, study, eat, watch television, and then go to bed. So, it was nice to be invited over to visit with my two neighbors.

When his partner went to bed, I was encouraged to stay for another drink. I happily obliged. I was enjoying the visit and the beer when he asked me to stand up. His huge hands reached over and pulled my pants down and he held me tight. Why didn't I scream? I'll never know. It probably was because I was scared and embarrassed. He held me down and told me that I needed what he was giving me. I struggled but could not get away. He was strong, big — and I was really scared. I don't know how long it lasted, but it seemed to be forever.

Afterward, I ran out of his apartment without saying a word. In my bedroom, I climbed into my bed — stunned. I don't think that I realized what had happened to me. I laid there in the darkness with my eyes wide open and several hours later finally fell asleep.

The next morning I woke up late feeling the same as when I went to bed. I cried and couldn't stop. I heard somebody knock at the door and went to answer it. It was my neighbor. He said that he was terribly sorry about what happened and he blamed it on his drinking. My feelings of self-hatred and disgust were beyond words, so I didn't say anything. I hated him. When he finished talking, I simply closed the door.

I got back into bed and stayed there almost all day. I felt lost and didn't know who to call. The feeling that I was at fault overtook me. How could I have let him do that to me? Why didn't I scream for help? Why didn't I tell him what I thought when he knocked at my door? I couldn't answer any of these questions. Hours went by as I lay in my bed and wept.

Several days later I called Washington D.C's Whitman-Walker Clinic for help. What happened to me was almost unbearable and I needed somebody to talk to. The clinic put me in touch with a counselor who charged me $45 per session. It was a lot of money to me because I was trying to make ends meet working during the day and studying for a degree at night. I went to therapy every week for several months. I found it almost impossible to talk about it. After several months and after spending quite a lot of money, I stopped going — mostly because I just couldn't afford it any longer.

Now, two years later, ... I have since moved and can hardly remember living in the old apartment. Before I moved from the apartment, I would sleep almost constantly. I guess I was in a state of depression.

Believe me, what happened to me screwed me up for a long time. Before the attack, I was reasonably self-confident. Today I am not so self-assured. I don't feel attractive at times and I sometimes feel dirty. Not a day goes by without thinking about the attack. The feelings of helplessness are overwhelming. The thoughts keep going through your mind that you could have made things different, but you didn't. The complete oblivion of self-confidence — it can overwhelm your entire life.

Rob's account of his experience gives us one limited look at the devastatation that abuse and violence leaves in its wake. If you reflect back on the reactions of most victims — confusion, helplessness, terror, vulnerability, anger, guilt, depression, meaninglessness, self-doubt, regret, as well as self-blame and self-hatred — you can see them all in Rob. There were also the unanswered questions that, like many other victims, may never get answered.

As we are finding out, many rapes occur in prison, and there is no crying out. Prison rape victims are left with the same excruciating reactions that are found in those outside of prison. And they face even fewer resources for help than those on the outside.

Another clear and powerful example of the potentially devastating effects of being victimized can be seen in Gary Geiger's experience. However, the outcome of Gary's experience is much more hopeful. I met Gary at Sing Sing. We were both invited to Sing Sing to offer presentations at the graduation of a year-long Victim/Offender Program.

In 1981, Gary was shot in a robbery at a Best Western Hotel in

Albany, New York where he worked nights as a financial auditor. At 3 A.M. four men entered the hotel, ordered Gary to lie on the floor, and demanded the key to the cash register. With fists and guns they beat him to the floor. As the men were leaving, Gary heard a shot. It was the sound of a .22-caliber handgun that punctured his lung and broke two ribs. Remains of the bullet are still lodged in his abdomen today. At the time of the shooting Gary was a thirty-four year old nationally ranked sprinter and power lifter. For someone who was in peak physical condition, the shooting was more than debilitating. His athletic carreer came to a halt.

After the robbery, Gary started having nightmares. He would find himself pacing the floor in a cold sweat night after night. He erupted in outbursts of rage at situations that would not have bothered him previously. He was depressed, angry, and anxious. He was fired from his job. Having almost no money, he lost his apartment and moved into a YMCA. He tried to see a psychiatrist, but no one would see him because he had no money or insurance. While all this was going on, the robbers were appearing in his dreams. Based on these dreams, he was able to identify two of the men in mug shots. A third man was later identified. All were arrested. With Gary's testimony (which he described as being more traumatic than the robbery) Wayne, the man who shot him, was given a twelve to twenty-five year sentence. The conviction gave Gary some relief.

After a long period of physical recuperation, Gary found another job and resumed some athletic training, but his anxiety and depression persisted. He flew into fits of rage at the slightest provocation. Eleven years after the shooting, like many victims of crime (and veterans of war), Gary was still suffering from Post Truamatic Stress Disorder.

In 1992 Gary saw an HBO documentary about a mediation between a schoolteacher and the teenager who beat him with a bat. Gary was so moved by what he saw that it started him on a mission to arrange a mediation between him and the man who shot him. He contacted Tom Christian, the director of the states Community Dispute Resolution Centers Program and requested a meeting. Although the Center did not usually mediate disputes in situations where there was "serious violence or injury," sensing Gary's sincere desire for reconciliation rather than revenge, Tom decided to contact Wayne to see if he would agree to meet the man he had shot. Wayne agreed.

At the time of the robbery (which netted $150) Wayne was twenty-one. He was a high school drop-out who had already served thirty-four months for robbery and a year for parole violations. He had been out of prison for four months when he met up with his friends the morning of the shooting. Until Tom Christian's call, Wayne had given little thought to the man he had shot. He said, "I had thought about what I had done to (Gary), but I didn't know this man except for that night, the robbery."

When Wayne was first approached about the meeting he was skeptical. He thought the mediation was a gimmick that would be used against him at the parole board. "But after talking to Mr. Christian," he said, "I figured it would help Mr. Geiger put it behind him, and it would give me a chance to speak to Mr. Geiger to see how this affected him."

Gary said, "I had a plan. I wanted him to talk about that day. I wanted answers to questions like, Why did he shoot me? Why did it get so violent? Did he try to kill me? The big goal for me was to get an apology. To me, a survivor of violent crime, an apology could be very profound. It would bring closure and healing. I wasn't going to ask for an apology. I wasn't going to beg for an apology. If it came, it came."

Unlike Gary, Wayne did not prepare what he would say. He wasn't going to explain or justify his actions. He was simply going to listen to what Gary had to say. His only plan was to apologize.

In the meeting, Gary explained to Wayne how he (Wayne) had been part of Gary's life for eleven years and how he wanted some honest answers. "He was making me see what I had done," Wayne said. "I didn't realize what I had done. I felt terrible. It wasn't something I'd want people to do to me."

When Wayne started to apologize, Gary started to cry. He said, "For eleven years I'd built this man up into a monster. Now he's just a human being. I thanked him. I said it takes a man to apologize." The session closed with a handshake.

From watching the unedited videotape of the meeting which Gary lent me, it seemed clear to me that the meeting had a significant healing effect on both men. Wayne was able to see, for the first time, the real human consequences of his actions. He was able to face up to what he had done and face the person he had done it to. As in true accountability, he was willing and able to help repair the damage.

When a people understand the hurt that they have caused, the real human suffering that is involved, they are more likely to be discouraged from repeating the behavior. If we hurt someone, it is important for us to understand, in as full a way as possible, what this has meant to the other person and our role in it. We need to look to see if there are ways we can take responsibility for our actions and make amends.

The outcome of Gary and Wayne's story is much happier than that of most victims and victimizers. Gary was a big-hearted man and both Gary and Wayne were willing to be courageous and honest, creating the space for healing to occur. They were given the rare opportunity to participate in what is referred to as restorative justice.

Unfortunately, the present system of criminal justice does not encourage mediation for those who are ready and would benefit from it. It seeks to keep victim (or in the case of murder, the victim's family) and offender apart, discouraging any kind of reconciliation or restitution. Of course there are offenders who are not willing to own their part and victims who are too scared, wounded, and angry to want any thing to do with the offender. Yet when the victim is open to some movement toward reconciliation and wants some answers, there is no way to get them. When an offender is truly remorseful and wants to stand accountable, there is most often no opportunity for the victim or the victims family to know this. The current retributive model of justice is interested in determining guilt and administrating punishment. Its' concern is not healing. The existing system inhibits closure for both victim and offender and in so doing, often keeps them linked together forever in unhealthy ways.

The rare exception to this is a small number of victim/offender programs that are being facilitated in prisons around the country. They are supervised meetings that usually bring together a small group of selectively-screened violent offenders and victims of violent crime. The purpose and hope of these meetings is that through open communication the offended parties might get some answers and begin some closure on the anger and pain they experience, and the offenders receive a realistic sense of accountability, separate from the physical reality of their prison sentence. In the process, each may find a new awareness, a point from which healing can occur. Studies have indicated that in addition to helping each to heal emotionally, both victims and offenders begin to break down stereotypes of the other. This restorative model of justice views crimes as being against people and the community and not the state. It is interested in solutions that promote repair, reconciliation, and reassurance.

Non-Violent Crimes

Even crimes that are considered "non-violent" can leave tremendous fear and devastation in their wake.

An extremely loving seventy-two year old woman comes to mind. Her home was robbed during the day when she was out taking care of a grandchild. Perhaps that robber rationalized his or her behavior by thinking, "No one was home so it was okay, and besides insurance will take care of the damages." Now this woman never feels safe in her home, and her fear propels her to spend every weekday wandering around shopping malls until her husband comes home from work. Every day her life is dominated by the fear of a "non-violent" robbery that happened three years before. She doesn't feel safe in her own home, even though it is in a neigborhood with a low crime rate. As is often the case, the psychological effect of the robbery was far more destructive than the material loss.

Even crimes that are considered non-violent in our legal system are laced with psychic violence against people. If we are honest with ourselves, we need to acknowledge this fact.

I think of people I have met, in and out of prison, who have sold cocaine to support their habit. They were selling cocaine to emotionally troubled fourteen and fifteen year olds. No one at fourteen or fifteen years old who is doing coke isn't troubled. And yet we call it "non-violent." We all need to look from the vantage point of the love, wisdom and integrity of the Self and from *that* vantage point, consider whether our actions are non-violent.

Living honestly and responsibly is everyone's issue all the time — anything less is a form of violence, however subtle, against our heart and soul and the heart and soul of others.

Abusing Power and Control

PAUSE AND REFLECT

Have you or do you abuse power and control?
Reflect on the following:
   • *Do you use intimidation? Do you make people afraid by using a look, actions, or gestures; destroying property, displaying weapons?*
   • *Do you use emotional abuse? Do you put people down, calling them names, playing mind games, making them feel guilty, humiliating them?*
   • *Do you minimize, deny and blame? Do you deny abuse*

happened when it did, shifting responsibility and saying they caused it, acting like the abuse is no big deal?

• *Do you use coercion and threats? Do you make or carry out threats to do something to hurt a person, threatening to leave (ie. a spouse) and to commit suicide, making a person do things they don't want to?*

• *Do you use "male privilege"? Do you treat others like servants, acting like the "master," defining roles in a relationship?*

• *Do you use isolation? — Do you control what another does, who they see and talk to, where they go, or use jealousy to justify actions?*

• *In domestic situations do you use children — use them to relay messages, threaten to take the children away (when it's not in the childrens' best interest), use visitation to harass a spouse?*

These abuses of power and control are used in domestic violence as well as physical and sexual violence toward others.

• *Do you use the alternatives to the abuse of control and power? What would it feel like if you treated everyone you met with honor and respect regardless of their position in life or personal history?*

• *Do you use non-threatening behavior? Are you respectful toward others? Are you honest and accountable for your actions?*

• *Do you use fairness and negotiation in settling disputes?*

• *Rather than using "male privilege" do you share responsibility?*

• *Rather than using isolation or control do you use trust and support?*

When Healthy Guilt Becomes Unhealthy Guilt

Healthy guilt guides our conscience and helps us to recover the responsibility and power to act with respect and integrity. Yet guilt can become unhealthy when we get lost in it and use it to beat ourselves up repeatedly. Feelings of guilt and remorse may stay with us for a lifetime when we think of a certain person or incident. Yet, if we are to heal and move on, this guilt and remorse can't remain a *predominating* emotional force.

Unhealthy guilt sets up a conflict within us that operates like two boxers in a ring — one boxer lacking any wisdom or compassion and the other, the loser. Everytime the loser gets up, he is beaten down again, day after day, month after month, year after year, never having enough time or psychological space to effectively learn from the past. Experiencing unhealthy guilt inevitably leads to the repetitive self-judgment that you are bad or stupid. Like the boxers in the ring, one part of you is always beating yourself down and you never get the chance to stand up, learn from your mistakes, and become the healthy person you have the potential to become. Unhealthy guilt is the sure death of self-esteem.

If we don't become aware and learn from our experiences and participate in the process of forgiving ourselves, prolonged unhealthy guilt plays itself out in some way. An insidious aspect of unhealthy guilt is that rather than prompting us on to heal and change in a positive way, it creates a vicious cycle. The "guilty" self unconsciously demands punishment or a pay back for what was done, and then doles out the sentence in the form of unhappiness, depression, a chronic sense of unworthiness, or even physical and mental illness. In addition to turning inward, unhealthy guilt (and toxic shame) can also be projected outward as chronic anger and resentment towards others. Chronic projection of guilt and shame lends itself to a static view of the world as a hostile, frightening, and unfair place. When unhealthy guilt predominates, people often act out destructive behaviors to unconsciously punish themselves for the profound guilt they still feel; for instance, an ex-offender may feel compelled to commit another crime. Unhealthy guilt produces a state of tension and anxiety that needs discharge and this discharge often finds release in acts of violence.

As with everything, being aware is the first step to change. Being aware of habitually putting yourself down or beating yourself up is the first step to transforming unhealthy guilt. Then by learning to forgive yourself, you come to see your mistakes as fearful reactions and confused attempts to get the power or love you felt you lacked. Only self-forgiveness can truly heal toxic shame and unhealthy guilt. It allows you to learn from your past while reminding you of your inherent goodness in the present.

The Life Review

After reading three books by Dr. Raymond Moody, (*Life After Life* (which sold over 3 million copies), *Reflections on Life After Life*, and *The Light Beyond*) I began to wonder if at some point in time we are all required to look at our actions and their impact on others. I wonder if we are all required to look at what we might once have avoided. I don't suggest that you should necessarily accept or believe his findings, but Dr. Moody's work (which has been replicated by many other researchers) is very interesting and relevant to the subject of guilt and life changes.

Over the past twenty years, Dr. Moody has interviewed thousands of people who experienced "Near Death Experiences" (NDEs). These people were pronounced dead from accidents, heart attacks, or other causes and then they were resusitated. Or, they were people who in the course of accidents, severe injury, or illness came very close to physical death. Dr. Moody interviewed thousands of people from all walks of life who had Near Death Experiences and found that many reported a series of common experiences. They described being aware that they were out of their body (they could see their body as if floating above it) and at some point moving on through a dark tunnel into a bright light. Some describe being met by beings of light — "by a beautiful and intense luminescense that seemed to permeate everything". They then described being met by a supreme Being of Light. Whoever it was, this being radiated total love and understanding. Many people referred to this presence as God.

At that point, people went through a "life review." The life review is a three-dimensional review of every single thing the person had done in their lives. The person's whole life flashed in front of them. Moody describes that "in this situation, you not only see every action that you have ever done, but you also perceive immediately the effects of every single one of your actions upon the people in your life." One feels the sadness, pain, and hurt of the people they have harmed. One also feels the love and happiness of all acts of kindness that one has done. People reported that as they go through this review the Being holds them in unconditional love and helps them put all the events of their life in perspective. All the people who Moody interviewed who had a Near Death Expereince came away believing that the most important thing in their life is to love.

Moody wrote about a man named Nick as an example of how the NDE changes people. Nick was described as a con artist and criminal, who had done everything from defrauding widows to running drugs. Crime had given him "the good life" — lots of money, nice cars, new homes, and "no problem with his conscience to annoy him." His life changed after being struck by lightning and "killed" while golfing one day. In a NDE, Nick described being met by a being of light that he called God. He described being led through a life review. While recovering in the hospital he said that he felt the full effect of his life review. At the same time, he experienced being "exposed to pure love." As with all people who have NDEs, Nick was transformed in a very deep and positive way. With no reservations, he left the life of crime behind and took on "an honest and helpful profession." Two of the things most commonly stressed by people like Nick who had a NDE were love and learning from one's experience.

I encourage you not to wait for death to knock at your door but to review your life now. Look back and acknowledge how your actions have affected others, both negatively and positively and, most importantly, be open to what you can learn from this. As you review your life, try to be gentle with yourself. If you have hurt others, it may be very difficult to look at how your actions have affected others without strong feelings of self-condemation and self-hatred. See if you can condemn the action while trying to keep your heart open with some mercy toward yourself. See if you can sense the powerlessness, fear, and desperation that underlies the abuse of power. If you can, I encourage you to imagine a Being of Light offering you unconditional love as you review your past.

EXERCISE

Reviewing Your Life

Get comfortable and take four long, slow, letting-go breathes. Give yourself some time to relax your mind and body. Then think back on acts of kindness and love that you have offered others — any small acts of kindness or love are fine. Recall how you felt in the moments of extending kindness or love. Recall how your kindness affected others. Enjoy the feeling. Notice how your body feels as you reflect on your kindness. Remember to breathe fully. Appreciate yourself for those acts of kindness and generosity.

Now, keeping your heart open to yourself, review the insensitive and hurtful things you have done in your life. (Perhaps you can call a Being of Light, A Higher Power, or any loving presence to support you. Feel the mercy and unconditional love that is totally natural for them to exude. Even if you have never felt it before, allow yourself to feel Their love now. It is there for you!) Breathe in and feel the wholeness within your own being. Sense the compassion and love of your deepest Self empowering you to see the truth during your review. Imagine this process as a turning point in your life as you review your whole life and learn as you have never learned from it before.

If you have ever been abusive or violent toward anyone, think about the impact that your abusiveness may have had (and may have) on that person, their family and their community. Bathed in the light and love of A Higher Source, allow yourself to see and learn from what you see.

Thank yourself, appreciate yourself for having the courage to heal.

* * *

CHAPTER 12

Self-Forgiveness: The Heart of Healing

George   I am a person who committed a crime against another person. Even though I've been in for thirteen years I don't have bitter or angry feelings about being locked up for what I did, because I know I was guilty, and I deserve punishment. I not only felt guilt, but I felt remorse, shame, and embarrassment for hurting another person. I became aware that my behavior had affected a lot of other people, not just the victim, but that person's family and friends as well as my own family and friends, not to mention my own life. For the first time in my life, I felt suicidal. I felt that I didn't deserve to live. I was a nothing. I didn't even have the courage to commit suicide, so I had to struggle with my feelings of self worth. At the time, I considered it courage, but now I realize that suicide would have been a coward's way out of having to deal with feelings.

I tried working hard to take care of the people who loved me. This gave me a feeling of value and self respect. It was a starting point for rebuilding my low self-esteem. During this time, I was involved with various forms of psychotherapy. In my therapy, I dealt with my relationships and my feelings. I sifted through every aspect of my life. I did this over and over again to try to find the answers that would help the feeling of unsettleness inside.

A person I had met through a business transaction while incarcerated, started to visit me on a regular basis. This turned into a friendship that I cherish to this day. A few years later, I was out on a visit with my friend. We were discussing and sharing thoughts and feelings when suddenly my friend said to me, "You've done so much and have made so many changes in your life. You're a good person, and you are my friend, so I need to say this to you. Forgive yourself." My friend repeated it again to make sure I heard what she had said.

Hearing those words was truly the beginning of my life. It was the beginning of a kind of change I never believed possible. As I write this, tears of happiness and love flow from my eyes in gratitude for two words no one had ever said to me before. "Forgive yourself." These were the two words I needed to hear and feel and put into practice in my life along with all the other therapeutic work to feel settled inside.

THE IDEA OF prisoners forgiving themselves is as unacceptable to many as the actual commission of a crime. Many people believe guilt and the threat of additional punishment are the driving forces that will stop future violence and criminal behavior. But as history has shown us, this threat doesn't work. Despite the profound sense of guilt and shame that many inmates feel, recidivism rates are high. Ironically, it is often a pervading sense of unhealthy guilt and shame that fuels violence and ensures a poor self-concept and low self-esteem. It is self-forgiveness that creates or restores this sense of self-esteem. Self-forgiveness is the heart of the healing process and, in my opinion, the only sure deterrent to crime.

Self-forgiveness, like all healing, is a process — not a one-time event. It is not a superficial act of saying, "Yeah, I did such and such, now I'll forgive myself." In many cases, true self-forgiveness takes time, courage, and a depth of honest looking that not everyone is ready or willing to do. Few people have an understanding of what it means to forgive themselves and, without question, prisoners have not been offered the necessary guidance and support. In fact, the prison experience undermines the process of self-forgiveness on a daily basis. Interaction after interaction fosters shame and reinforces the self-concept of the prisoner as an inferior person who has not been forgiven and who will never be forgiven.

When I first bring up the issue of self-forgiveness many people think that it is not for them. Their limited or mis-understanding of self-forgiveness makes it impossible. Not understanding what self-forgiveness is, many people feel there is no way they could ever forgive themselves — or be forgiven.

If you are open and patient, and sincerely work with the concepts and exercises in this chapter, then regardless of your past, the freedom and peace of self-forgiveness are within your reach.

What Self-forgiveness Is Not

Before getting into how to actually forgive yourself, let's start by clearing up some misconceptions about self-forgiveness. Let's start by being clear about what self-forgiveness *is not*.

Self forgiveness is *not* re-defining an offense as a non-offense. It is not condoning behavior that is hurtful, insensitive, abusive, or that lacks integrity. It is not excusing or overlooking it. It is not diminishing the importance or impact of your actions. Doing any of these is rationalization, denial, and self-deception.

Self-forgiveness is *not* absolving yourself of responsibility or acting like everything is okay when it isn't. Part of self-forgiveness is taking full responsibility for your role in whatever has happened. All of this is true for everyone — whether their guilt is in relation to a serious crime or a minor incident.

Self-forgiveness should *never* be equated with avoidance of guilt or remorse for the past. In fact, feeling remorse and regret for pain that one has caused or for bad decisions one has made is part of the healing process.

Self-forgiveness is *not* taking a righteous attitude and saying "I forgive myself because God or Jesus (or whomever) has forgiven me — when, in truth, you haven't done the inner work and soul-searching that is necessary for inner healing. Rather than being genuine self-forgiveness, this kind of thinking is a cop-out.

If you feel connected spiritually, your relationship with a higher power may provide the unconditional love that helps to empower you to forgive yourself. But as Bill's experience conveys, you must still do your own part.

Bill I continued to run from myself and blame everything on others and continued to hate myself. I attempted suicide several times and I've been in and out of jail and prison since I was 13 years old. I used every kind of drug there is to try to hide. I was an alcoholic and a dope addict but it only helped temporarily. I continued down my path of self destruction until I killed an innocent woman and ended up on death row. Well I got in a position where I couldn't run anymore. The guilt and hatred really went to work on me then. I continued to run from myself and I didn't want to face up to what I had done. I knew what I had done and I felt so bad for it but I knew there was nothing I could do to change it. It all finally piled up on me so much that I couldn't deal with it anymore. I accepted Jesus Christ in my life and I started to look at things a lot different. I still struggled along and I finally stepped back and took a good long look at where I was and started looking over everything I had done in my life. I could see all the pain I had caused my own family, people I loved and people I didn't even know. I felt the Lord leading me to see what I needed to do in order for me to accept forgiveness. First I had to forgive myself. In order for me to do that I had to accept responsibility for my own actions. That was hard. I didn't want to be responsible for everything I had done. I didn't want to be the monster everyone said I was.

Well after much self examination I finally could see where things started to go wrong in my life and I could see where it was my own choices and my own action that did all the bad things. No one forced me to do anything. I know I was on drugs and an alcoholic but I still had to accept responsibility for my own actions. Since I have accepted responsibility for what I have done I have, with the help of God, forgiven myself and I know that God has forgiven me. I can look in the mirror without having hatred for the face I see looking back at me now. I have peace inside for the first time in my life.

Bill discovered that when he accepted Jesus into his life, the personal inner work was not done for him. But he was given the direction, courage, and inner strength to do what was needed to heal. Unless we do this work, God's unconditional love is usually experienced as a theory or concept rather than as a direct and profoundly liberating experience.

The Steps of Self-forgiveness

You will notice as you read through the following "steps of self-forgiveness," that they have all been addressed at some length in earlier chapters. If you have been working with the exercises up to this point, you have already established a firm foundation for self-forgiveness.

The process of self-forgiveness is highly individual. How long it will take to work on each of the steps varies from person to person. Some steps may need months or years to be processed. Others may take minutes. The steps of self-forgiveness are not distinct units, but rather have overlapping boundaries.

STEP 1. ACKNOWLEDGING THE TRUTH

The act of acknowledging the truth refers not only to the truth of what you have done but also to the truth about your feelings and the truth about how your actions have affected others.

Acknowledging the entire truth of our experience takes courage. It takes courage to accept the fear, humiliation, shame, sadness, self-hatred, and the actions, inner thoughts, and feelings that a part of us would rather repress and avoid.

Rather then being an easy way out of confronting your past, self-forgiveness calls for total confrontation. As noted in the last chapter, if you committed an offense against an individual, you need to challenge yourself to come to as full an understanding as possible of what your actions have meant to the victim, his or her family, and the community.

Whenever possible, get into an offender specific group. (If you are a sex offender, get into a group that deals with the issues that are specific to sex offenders; If you are a batterer, get into a group for batterers; etc.) These groups offer a unique opportunity to acknowledge and face the issues specific to the offense. Whatever your offenses, you have to get down and dirty about what you have done and how it has affected everyone, including yourself and your own family — again, *not* so that you can beat yourself up but so you can heal. To deny the truth is to deny yourself the possibility of healing.

The fifth step in the twelve-step program of Alcoholics Anonymous is: "We admitted to God, to ourselves, and to another human being the exact nature of our wrongs." By acknowledging your mistakes and transgressions to another, you actively support the process of healing and letting-go. By sharing the things about which you feel badly with a compassionate person, you help lift the heavy burden of guilt. Telling the whole truth to another can be terrifying, making you feel very vulnerable and open to rejection. Yet often the fear around sharing your darkest truth with another dissolves as you find that telling it brings relief. As author Mark Matousek wrote,

"To confess is to take possession of your life at last." As you allow yourself to confess the truth and share your pain, guilt and shame, you give up sole possession of these feelings. You end the state of isolation that guilt often imposes and restore a sense of connection with other people, humanity, and the unity of all life. You find you are still acceptable, and you create more room in your heart for yourself.

Frank When I begin to acknowledge the truth, the feelings of remorse, regret, pity, and sorrow start to creep from the emotional woodwork. These are real and powerful emotions that must be dealt with. When they cropped up in the past, I would bury their bones with the distorted pleasure of drug abuse. Now they are unburied and rearing up from the graveyard of the past and have to be dealt with and used in a positive way.

Pat At first I found this the most difficult of all the steps to accept and achieve. Feelings of guilt and shame occurred almost instantly when I faced the truth. However, I knew that without confronting the truth I would always carry a burden within me. Somehow I finally felt the need to face the truth and once I did, I felt as if I was set free and there was nothing that I could not face.

PAUSE AND REFLECT

Reflect back on your life. How have your choices and actions affected you and others. If you committed a crime in which there were victims, imagine how the victim(s) felt during the crime. Imagine how the victim(s) and their families and friends are affected now. Put yourself in their shoes.

Acknowledge the truth of your actions and feelings.

Reflect back on the fifth step of Alcoholics Anonymous and let yourself take this step.

STEP 2. TAKING RESPONSIBILITY
FOR WHAT YOU HAVE DONE

Taking responsibility for what we have done requires that we stop blaming others and making excuses for our own behavior. It requires honestly answering to ourselves and others in relation to what has happened and repairing the damage in whatever ways we can.

An important part of taking responsibility, one also in keeping with the Twelve-step programs, is making amends when possible.

Ed This is a difficult step for many of us to accept. I too have blamed drug abuse for my problems, but no more! Nobody put a gun to my head to force me to take drugs. I often blame a car accident I was in for my experiencing so much regret, doubt in my self, and fear but I'm through making excuses for myself. I have no blame to spread around anymore, as I once did. It was much easier to dull my fears and pain with hard drugs, but actually my fears have not eased any after all the drugs. Now I have attracted even more difficulties to deal with. I now realize it must all be dealt with from within. It must be done honestly, without fear of the consequences. Fears are only thoughts. I feel a great sense of relief in accepting all of this.

Rita My choices — some good, but many bad, were my choices. They made me who I am today and will make me into who I'll be tomorrow. I realize that responsibility is more than just admitting to the wrongs I've done. I am responsible for all aspects of my life... what I say, the behaviors I exhibit, along with my well being. By keeping this in the forefront of my mind I stop myself from blaming others for what happens to me.

PAUSE AND REFLECT

List the ways that you could take responsibility for what you have done.

Then look over your list and start to follow through in whatever ways you can.

<hr />

STEP 3. LEARNING FROM EXPERIENCE
BY ACKNOWLEDGING THE DEEPER FEELINGS
THAT MOTIVATED BEHAVIORS
FOR WHICH YOU NOW FEEL GUILTY

Because the vast majority of inmates are brought up in dysfunctional homes where emotional abandonment and abuse are common, rather than being in touch with your intrinsic worth and value, there is a good chance you grew up feeling insecure and inadequate. It is this unresolved pain and toxic shame that usually fuel the sense of powerlessness that leads to drug abuse and the abuse of power.

As part of the process of self-forgiveness it is essential to step back and take an honest, objective look at the people and circumstances that influenced the thoughts and feelings that you now have about yourself. By becoming aware of these influences, you can begin to develop greater understanding and compassion for yourself. You can see that you were not a bad person making bad choices, but a fundamentally good person who because of unresolved pain, anger, and insecurity, acted destructively.

The inner child work is a powerful means for this healing. By reflecting on the experiences and feelings of the inner child, you gain insight into how these experiences have influenced your self-image, self-esteem, feelings, and behaviors as an adult. In order to fully experience the peace of self-forgiveness, it is crucial to work on healing these emotional wounds.

Ralph Part of facing the truth meant I had to look at all the horrific abuse that others have inflicted on me when I was a child. In this process I learned the truth of what I was not responsible for and that I was not born a bad person. Most of what I blamed myself for was truly not my fault. And finally facing the truth of what I was and am responsible for — i.e. how my actions effect others and myself.

Until recently most of the truths I had to face were extremely painful. Today I struggle to really accept the wonderful and good Self I am and always had been.

Victor   Today I'm more aware than ever of my unresolved pain and low self-esteem. Going back in honesty and seeing hurt, abuse, and the lack of warmth and comfort when I needed to be comforted has helped me to understand my feelings of powerlessness and inferiority. It's now easy to see why I never felt whole. Going back in the inner child work has started a healing of those hurts. I know I still have lots of work ahead. I understand I'm on a journey that will take me through my pain and fear but I feel it will eventually bring about emotional and spiritual healing and finally self forgiveness and wholeness once again.

PAUSE AND REFLECT

Go back through your childhood, as far back as you can remember until about age sixteen. Try to recall how you felt as a child during various ages and how you were treated by the people who were important to you. As you do this keep in mind that the core Self was never affected by any of this. Now think of some of the things you did in your life for which you now feel guilty. Can you see how your childhood experiences influenced your later experiences?

STEP 4. OPENING YOUR HEART TO YOURSELF

In keeping with the last step, self-forgiveness *requires* a certain degree of compassion and gentleness with yourself. This does not imply self-indulgence or lenience that excuses or absolves accountability. Sometimes true compassion requires "ruthless compassion," the willingness to be honest and accountable to yourself when it is extremely painful to do so. An open heart is the personal context that allows you to experience safety in honesty and vulnerability rather than the false safety many people have historically known through projection, denial, numbing, dishonesty, control, and manipulation.

It is a non-judging acceptance of true feelings that leads the way to the transformation of these feelings and to a new depth of emotional maturity. It is through gentleness and compassion that you create the internal climate to reveal yourself to yourSelf, to allow your dark side to come into the light of awareness so that you can heal emotional wounds.

Sue This is what I should have done long ago. I have always been very hard on myself. But false pride stopped me. I'm confident that if I used my heart more and could let it guide me more, I'd be less fearful. It's such a relief to listen to your own heart.

Ralph By opening my heart to myself I get to know myself, my true self. By opening my heart to myself, I understand myself. I accept myself. I have love for myself. I feel hopeful. I must say pulling off my many masks and seeing the pain that created each one of them took a lot of painstaking work. But when I finally stood bare, and saw myself a wave of emotion and joy and peace and understanding swept me to my knees. There before me stood the honest, loving, creative, and understood Self. "Free."

Hakeem I feel that opening my heart to myself allows me to see deep inside myself to a place I seldom knew until now. I feel I have to be loving and gentle with myself but practice "tough love" with my bad habits. There's no need to punish myself. Only compassion can allow me to change my behavior. It's time to be kind and nurturing to myself so that my true Self can emerge and take over where the false selves once ruled.

PAUSE AND REFLECT

How are you hard on yourself? About what issues and behaviors do you judge yourself to be inferior or bad? How do you punish yourself? Try to see beyond this "crime and punishment" self-image to the part of yourself that is always loving and always deserving of love.

STEP 5. HEALING EMOTIONAL WOUNDS BY HEEDING THE INNER CALLS FOR LOVE IN HEALTHY AND RESPONSIBLE WAYS

Any self-destructive act or emotion can be understood as a call for help and love. In addition to working on the preceding steps, heeding these calls takes the willingness to be there for yourself in a variety of nurturing ways. Some of these ways include getting support from skilled and caring counselors, therapists, clergy, etc.; attending support groups; choosing not to associate with people who have a negative influence on you and choosing to associate with people who are a positive influence; reading books that are educational and inspiring; exercising; meditating; and praying.

Carlos After 25 years I can finally say I'm now giving my full attention to this inner call for love. I believe I've drunk, drugged, run, and hid for fear of answering this call all these years. I've heard the call many times, but that negative side yelled, "DON'T". It convinced me I wasn't worthy of being good and loving to myself. I now know better and am getting the guidance I need. My reading, study of scripture, and meditation have transformed my life.

PAUSE AND REFLECT

What are four ways that you can nurture your growth and well-being? Make a list.

Clearly you are already doing one important thing by reading this book. If you are not already doing it, choose at least one other way to nurture yourself and give yourself the gift of doing it today.

STEP 6. ALIGNING WITH THE SELF AND AFFIRMING YOUR FUNDAMENTAL GOODNESS

When you begin to align with the Self, with your innate capacity for wisdom, compassion, and conscious choice, then there is growing self-respect, a healthier sense of responsibility toward yourself and others, courage, and a belief in your ability to meet life's challenges. By aligning with the Self you are increasingly able to see when an inner self-critic keeps you locked in humiliation, unhealthy guilt and shame, and locked out of your own heart. The more you align with the Self, the more you will offer yourself gentleness and as a result, the more you will learn and grow from your experiences. The more you will feel the strength and inspiration you need to keep the process of self-healing and self-forgiveness on sure footing. When you align with the Self you naturally experience greater peace and hopefulness and you access the inclination and power to live with greater love.

Rita This to me is the reward for honestly committing myself to change. It is reinforced with my daily contact with God. When we align with our Self through prayer and meditation we can see this person that God created and not the person that we created. This alignment with Self brings about the knowledge and awareness that the present is where we should be living and each moment contains a choice as to how we shall be in it. I now trust my inner Self to speak to me when I begin to falter or when a decision is needed. It always leads us correctly.

Joe All of the steps that I've been working on couldn't have taken place without getting in touch with myself. Getting in touch with my inner self allows me to see the world in a broader and less constricted way. It allows me the choice of what I want to participate in. "Self" allows me to think and analyze circumstances and make choices rather than constantly committing to impulsive and spontaneous reactions. Self allows me to realize that I am worth something and can succeed at the things I choose.

PAUSE AND REFLECT

Recall a situation that you feel guilty about. Take some time to reflect on what motivated your behavior. What can you presently learn about yourself from that experience? With this new awareness, how could you behave differently if you encounter a similar situation in the future? Breathe in and feel the wholeness within your own being. Imagine yourself in a similar situation responding with clarity and dignity.

Bring other situations that you feel guilty about to mind. Do this exercise over with each of them.

Completion and Closure

When you align with your Self and discover the basic goodness of your own true nature, your consistent inclination will be to live with honesty and integrity. You will want to create closure or completion with any unfinished business from the past and actively make amends when it is possible and appropriate to do so; this may be in relation to a victim of crime, an old friend, an acquaintance, or a family member.

All forgiveness implies some completion. Completion is coming to as much closure with issues as possible. It is a healing or letting go. If you have unfinished business and you haven't done what is in your power to bring closure to it, inner conflict and uneasiness are apt to arise each time you think about the people or circumstances involved.

There are many ways to foster completion within yourself and in relationships. These include confessing or telling the truth, apologizing, asking for forgiveness, doing some sort of selfless service. Sometimes completion happens just by seeing yourself and others in the light of a new understanding.

Forgiving yourself and others may not require that you do or say something beyond your own inner process of healing and letting go. There may be times when you think, "I need to talk with X in order to clear the air." But the other person may be dead, unreachable, or not interested in talking or hearing from you. In order not to get permanently stuck in the past, in anger and unhealthy guilt, you must adjust what you think you need to do to what is possible. And, there are times when things may be better left unsaid. Be careful though, not to choose silence as an escape from facing another when you know in your heart that being directly honest is possible, appropriate, and likely to be most healing.

APOLOGIZING

In many cases the best way to deal with someone you have wronged, or been insensitive to, is to straightforwardly acknowledge the truth and apologize. In some situations, especially those with victims of crime who you did not know, it may be inappropriate (or even illegal) to reach out. If you know communication from you is not welcome, it may be most respectful to leave the person alone. Some people may be relieved and welcome the opportunity to heal the relationship. This doesn't mean that you or they will necessarily resume an active relationship if you had one before. But it does mean that you can help release yourself and others from the painful past.

Apologizing can be very freeing, *but* it is freeing *only* if it is done from the heart and without any expectations. If you assume that your apology will be gladly accepted, you set yourself up for "getting an attitude" if your apology is not accepted. Remember that despite apologies, genuine remorse, and positive changes in your behavior — such as ceasing to do the things that evoked another's anger in the past — other people may still not be ready or willing to forgive. It is important that you are careful not to impose your need for completion on another person who doesn't want to engage. It is also important that you don't allow another's anger and fear to fan the fire of your own unhealthy guilt. Don't allow your self-forgiveness to be contingent on other people's readiness or willingness to forgive you. They may not be ready to let go of their anger. They may get something from holding on to the anger that they may never be willing or ready to let go of. They may be too frightened or wounded to let go of their anger. Feeling angry may be an important part of their process of healing at this time.

Allow others to be where they are. Respect their right to feel the way they feel. Only in accepting another's right to be where they are, can you nurture or maintain self-forgiveness for yourself. You may certainly have a desire for them to forgive you and respond differently, but recognize that you have the desire and let it be. When you get caught in wanting another person to change, you separate yourself from your Self, and necessarily experience guilt and anger again.

WRITING

Another useful way to support the completion process is to write a letter of apology or a letter simply sharing what the truth is for you. There may be many things you want to say to someone. Writing is a powerful way to clarify your thoughts and feelings. You may write it intending to send the letter. Even if this person is alive and available, you may choose not to send it if you sense he or she isn't open to hearing from you at this time. Or, there may be times when you feel guilty and remorseful, but sending the letter might compromise a third party — for instance, writing to someone's husband and telling him you are sorry you slept with his wife, when the wife has chosen not to tell her husband about it. Even if you throw the letter away or never send it, putting your feelings and thoughts into words on paper can move you further on the path of your own healing.

VISUALIZATION

Completion can also be aided by visualization. You can stop for a few minutes a day, imagine being with that person and with love in your heart ask for his or her forgiveness. Allow yourself to work on forgiving yourself even if you feel the person to whom you are apologizing is still angry. See if you can find it in your heart to wish them well even if they don't wish you the same.

ACTS OF SELFLESS SERVICE

Another way to move toward completion is through acts of selfless service. If you search your soul and you find that you've taken away or deprived someone of something of value to them (i.e. a person's freedom, self-respect, trust, innocense, material property, or physical well-being), you may want to offer re-payment in the form of selfless service. Selfless service is service where you don't do it for personal acknowledgment or gain. You don't do it in order to get points for good behavior. You do it to pay back what you've taken in some way, (even if it's not directly to the person you've wronged.) You do it to heal yourself. Acts of this kind can be any work that makes someone else's well-being your priority.

Failing Yourself

Some of the things for which you blame yourself may not be things that you think of as ethically wrong, but rather you judge as stupid, thoughtless, impulsive, or weak. "I can't believe I did that! I must have been spineless." "What a fool I am." "I sold out on my-self again." Actions and decisions that might provoke that kind of reaction may include having been part of an abusive relationship, never doing things that you've always wanted to do, or doing things you didn't want to do, being addicted to something or someone you know is hurtful. You may even resent yourself for being afraid to make a change and hate yourself for feeling helpless and hurt.

You may think that mentally beating yourself up will motivate you to change or live up to your true potential. Chronic unhealthy guilt and self-blame can seem to serve as the constant nagging that we need to wake ourselves up, yet they actually lull us to sleep keeping the power to heal ourselves inactive.

You may wonder how we can trust ourselves to make thoughtful, loving, and appropriate choices if we don't judge ourselves and others. We have been conditioned to believe that our judgments are necessary, that they have value. It is common to believe that if we didn't judge ourselves we would act unethically, never change for the better and be lazy slobs. Our ego assures us that our judgments will keep us in line. But quite to the contrary, it is the undermining nature of our chronic self-judgments that keep us stuck in an often vicious cycle of act and remorse. What these judgments really do is keep us out of our own heart and separate from the clarity, love and natural integrity that is our deepest inclination and highest need to express.

EXERCISE

Becoming Your Own Friend

To begin, take four deep letting-go breaths. With each out-breath, feel your body relaxing.

Imagine what it would be like to live with someone who constantly judges you as wrong, bad, weak, or stupid for the things you have done and do. This would, in all likelihood, undermine the confidence and/or motivation to make the changes you want.

Now imagine instead, that you make choices that are not what you really want for yourself and that you live with a kind, wise, and insightful person who can clearly see when you make those choices. But instead of emotionally and mentally beating you down for them, this person offers you love and acceptance. At the same time, this person helps you to look at your choices with a new clarity, compassion and wisdom.

Imagine that this kind person supports you in seeing the fears and conditioning that motivate you. S/he understands that your choices, even self-destructive ones, were attempts to find relief, power, peace, and happiness. This person knows, and wants you to know, that the choices you made that were harmful to yourself and others were a result of the fear and separation from yourSelf that you were experiencing. S/he assures you that there are other choices you can make now. This person encourages you to open to and accept support from a higher power, and from others. S/he tells you that you can heal, that there is truly grace in your life, and that only you can let it in........

Go back over the last two paragraphs and imagine what it would be like if you befriended yourself in this same way. Repeat this suggestion many times in the days ahead. Become a true friend to yourself.

* * *

Sam For as long as I can remember I have acted on impulse, without regard for consequences, not looking beyond short range gratification. Being my own best friend is just another way of saying awareness, will, and choice.

Joe Before incarceration I was functioning only through my subpersonalities and, as a result, did not allow myself to become my own friend. I had no compassion for myself. The only thing that I allowed was constant punishment and criticism of myself. Whenever I had a chance, I would badger myself about all of the negative choices I had made and forgot about all of the good things that I had done. Instead of being my own best friend, I had in fact, become my own worst enemy. I was totally disgusted with myself. I had beat myself up both physically and mentally more than anyone could have ever done.

When I leave the system, I know that I will not be the same person that came into the system. I realize I don't have to wait to be released to see how different things can be. Things are different for me now. I have taken the initiative to become my own best friend while incarcerated and have found myself progressing very rapidly as a result. I have taken advantage of the time that I have had to analyze my past, present, and future. I have had time to think about what life is worth to me and what I want out of life. I now know that there will be times where I will be the only friend that I have and I can still make it through trials and tribulations, no matter what they are or what the outcome may be. I know that strength comes from within and it is my choice of how much I wish to exercise that inner strength.

When you step back, use insight, and look at yourself with discriminating wisdom, rather than judging yourself as being basically bad or stupid, you begin to see clearly what motivated you to make the choices that you made. In order to stop the cycle of chronic self-judgment, and the self-punishment that follows, you must offer yourself greater compassion — even while feeling shame, guilt, anger, grief, and pain. Rather than beating yourself up for where you are or what you have done, you can begin working with the steps of self-forgiveness so that you can learn from your experiences and emotionally heal and mature.

*If you find that you are unwilling to consider forgiving yourself
now, contemplate and complete the following:*

Notice your responses with a gentle non-judging awareness.

I am not willing to forgive myself for_____.

What I get out of holding onto this self-condemnation is _____.

What I give up by holding onto this self-condemnation is ____.

Keep repeating these sentences until you have no more responses.

A Small Part of One Man's Journey

Although self-forgiveness can be described in terms of steps and
concepts, it comes about through the inner work we do on ourselves. This very small fragment of one man's journey toward self-
forgiveness powerfully shows us many of the important aspects of
this process.

The following letter was written by an inmate to his ex-wife after a great deal of self-reflection, aided by individual and group therapy sessions he had been attending in the prison.

Paul's Letter

Dear Mary,

The letter you are about to read is my personal history. I have
mixed feelings about letting you into my deep dark past. I value you
highly — your opinion, your friendship and love. I am so afraid! I feel
so ashamed of my own past and so vulnerable but I know that if I am
to help you understand why I acted the way I did I *must* tell you.

As you know, my family was not deprived — not of material
things. Sure I had plenty of clothes and toys, but I was deprived of
one major aspect of life...love. You have seen how my folks are. They

don't express love. They try to buy it. Well, they have been like this as long as I've known them.

I have a few memories of growing up and most of them cause nothing but pain. My earliest memories are of being tied to a tree in the backyard while mom cleaned the house. The house *had* to be clean — it was more important than I was. When I was 7 or 8 dad was chasing me and I crawled under his truck. I cut the shit out of my back, I was bleeding like a stuck pig. I went running to mom who was hanging laundry, and she said to me "Don't come crying to me" She had absolutely no sympathy.

I remember another time, thinking she would forgive me for swearing so I told her I swore and I was sorry. She dropped my pants right there and gave me a good beating. The thing that made it so hard was that I was outside with some of the kids from the neighborhood when I told her. She beat me in front of them. I was the joke of the neighborhood for months.

Then I was about 8 or 9 like most kids I was playing with matches. Me and David got caught lighting matches. David's mom yelled at him. Mine turned on the electric stove and kept my finger tips on the coils until my fingers *smoked*. I hated David for getting off so easy.

Then there are the memories of not going to school because I had been beaten and was all swolen. One time, the Sunday after Thanksgiving, mom and dad went up to see nana and grampa. I was babysitting. When they came home the phone rang. The operator said that someone at this number was making obscene phone calls. My dad asked us if we had done it and for some reason I laughed. That's all it took. I can remember me trying to run. He caught me by the hair and literally threw me *over* the dining room table. Needless to say I was out of school a couple of days. To this day I don't know if one of the kids had been making those phone calls. The whole time I was in school the only time I was out sick was once for the mumps the other times were for *stankings* as they used to call them.

The only thing I can remember about living at home was pain. When I was about 9 this guy who lived a few houses away started to make friends with me. He was in high school. He would have me sexually perform for him. He molested me, but I didn't think of it as bad because he gave me attention, which I thought was love.

Mare, now comes the hardest part yet. When I was young about 11 my cousin who I won't name used to baby sit me. She was older, maybe 19. She was my first lover. At first she had me fondle her breasts and she would get me to suckle on her. I remember her patting my head as I lay in her lap suckling. This relationship went on for almost four years. Mare, we ended up having a full sexual relationship. She lived next door which made it quite easy. Along with a sexual relationhip we also had a mother and son relationship. She became the mother I had never had. She knew when I was being punished and she would come visit me during the night.

I see now that whenever I had a girlfriend I tried to get adopted by her family. I also can see how I had to get physical to feel that I was communicating my feelings. Mare, you remember how much I hung around. That was because your family meant so much to me. I can't really describe the depth of my feelings towards your family, but I can honestly say I felt closer to your family in the short time I was a part of it than the life time I was with my own family.

As you know one of us got pregnant and both of us got scared! I remember your mother guessing you were pregnant and although she blew off steam she tried to be understanding. I also remember how my family reacted. Needless to say I never got any support from them and I hated them for that. We got a truck load of gifts but not an once of support.

I wanted our marriage to work *soo* bad!! I wanted to be a good husband and I wanted my child to have the best. Most of all I wanted her to *know* she was *loved*. Now that I look back I wanted to give her something I knew nothing about — *love*.

As our marriage went on you know how I got violent and beat you up. Then I said I was sorry. I was in so much turmoil. I didn't know how to communicate the anger or disappointment of the particular situation, so I struck out physically. I did realize I was converting to the violent attitude of my parents. *I was not going to let that happen!* I started saying I was sorry for everything even though down inside I wasn't sorry. I just didn't know how to talk about it.

Now comes the really scary part — scary for me. Please understand this has been ripping me apart for years.

When we moved to your mother's I was living in a world of depression. I saw the only world I felt like I fit into slowly decaying. Then came the night that started the down fall. I can't remember where you were, but Joanne [his daughter] did something that made me snap. *I hit her!*

In a matter of seconds I felt my whole world had crumbled. The family I was part of no longer accepted me. I couldn't handle the realization of the rejection, of loosing or admitting I had lost you and the family. After I hit her I didn't know what to do to tell her *I love you.* Mare, I fell back on what I had been taught — to love is to touch. So I took Jo out back and tried to show her I loved her and I was sorry by the only means I understood. After I had assaulted her I took her to McDonalds to buy her something, to *buy* her love like my folks had always done.

I can't tell you how ashamed I am. It wasn't until I saw how others perceived me that I realized how dirty and filthy I had acted. What I did was try to show the love of my life the purest sense of love I knew. I didn't mean it to be anything disgusting or filthy, to me I was saying *Joanne, I love you. Believe me!*

It took me almost two years just to be able to face myself — to be able to say it wasn't *all* my fault and that someone had helped me be this way. I don't know if I will ever forgive myself for what I did to Joanne. I realize I am taking a big gamble telling you all about me. I don't know how you will react, will this help you understand me? Will this help you to see me as a man who loves you and Joanne very much and is trying to find a way to be understood or (possibly) be forgiven?

Mare, I'm scared. I don't know if I will ever hear from you after reading this. I feel like I have ripped open my chest and are showing you all my scars and ugliness. and I'm standing here waiting to see if you scream at the ugliness. or will you possibly see me, the man trying to heal. I am a man who loves you two but didn't know how to express it. Please hear how sorry I am for all the pain I have caused. All I want is a chance to repair the damage.

Since I have been incarcerated I have learned more about myself. I admit to what I feel. I don't ignore it, I am honest to myself. I have developed this strange feeling called self-esteem. Before I didn't believe myself. My own opinion didn't mean a thing. Now I care about me. I am not afraid to say what I think. I have found *ME*.

I have found and destroyed the animal and saved the man. It's up to you whether or not you see that man.... It's up to you.

Paul's story demonstrates the boldness that is required to be honest, to ask for forgiveness and to forgive. And he asks, "How does the story of a person making these choices end?" The answer, "with *saving the man*." Each act of forgiving ourselves or others comes down to a choice that each of us must individually make. The bottom line is...., it is a personal choice.

How Long Does It Take To Forgive Yourself?

Like all forgiveness, self-forgiveness is a process. It's a path you travel, not a permanent state you reach. Sometimes people wonder "When will I ever forgive myself for things that are over and done? Will I ever really love myself?" Even when it comes to healing the more glaring guilt and shame, there is no set time that healing takes. Even a few minutes here and there when you feel more compassionate and loving towards yourself indicates there is healing and health. It is important to remember that growth happens in a spiral. The more you heal, the more you love and accept yourself, the more the subtler feelings of guilt, shame, and unworthiness can come to your awareness, to be owned and healed.

For some people it takes many years for certain wounds to fully heal. For others certain healing may take but a moment in time. There will be times when you can see or sense great progress — when you feel self-accepting, peaceful, and optimistic. There will also be times when you feel ashamed, embarrassed, self-critical and discouraged. The important thing to remember is that if you are willing to be more compassionate and more self-affirming, even though the connection to your Self will be lost and found again, and lost and found again, and lost and found again — it will be lost less and less. It will be found more and more.

EXERCISE

A Letter of Forgiveness to Yourself

After working with the six steps of self-forgiveness, as well as with the other exercises in this chapter, write a letter of forgiveness to yourself.

* * *

Barry...   Letter to myself This is a letter to myself and to all the other faces I have used over the years. You cannot forget all the misfortune of the past but you must not dwell in the past. You must find hope in the present and a purpose for the future. You must establish a goal for your existence, use all these old feelings in a new and positive way. Everyday you must remind yourself that you are a new and better person. I can not stress the importance of this enough. Everyday delusion will creep into your awareness. You must fight it off and look at your motivations. Remember where you have

been and think about where you are going before you head off. You
never did this before and you have a unique opportunity to see where
you once were blind, to bring sound from emotional silence, to experience feeling from numbness, and to find real love. You have
walked naked through the heart of darkness and survived.

Joe...   Letter to myself

Dear Joe,

What I am about to write pertains to you and the past experiences
that you have had. I know that you have caused a lot of emotional
harm to yourself as well as to others. I know that you wish you could
go back and undo all the wrongs that you have done. I know that you
suffer emotionally because your life has not gone "according to plan."
I know you've set goals in the past and abandoned them and when
you decided to pick them back up, it's been too late. I know how
you've been presently feeling about your incarceration and how you
feel about leaving your family. I know your pain. I know your hurt. I
am part of what you're feeling. This is the true you. This is really
what you've wanted. To feel true emotions again.

I know you've felt guilty about your past and present situations
but it's okay now. It's okay to feel guilt but it shouldn't be lingered in
throughout the rest of your life. You can forgive yourself for those
times. You didn't forget them or repeat them. You've held on to them
long enough to LEARN from them. Growth is the most important
aspect of making mistakes. You've done that. Now it's time to let go.
Without forgiveness, you prevent yourself from the growth that you
are capable of.

I know you've been working real hard with the new things that
you've learned and sometimes it's one hell of a struggle but that's
what makes the outcome of all your efforts that much sweeter. Continue to practice and implement the things that you have learned
into your life. Continue to face the issues that you have consistently
avoided all of these years. Continue to practice love, peace, and for-

giveness toward others. But the most important step for you is to forgive yourself about the past and continue to forgive yourself for mistakes to come. And, if it is of any value coming from me to you, I have forgiven you.

Love yourself because

I do,

Joe

Julio...   Letter to myself

Dear Self,

It's been a long, hard twenty or so years we've been through and we both understand so painfully well what a waste it's been. Every month, every year that passed only added to our grief and anger. Yes, it's been rough, but maybe there is an end at hand. It's even a relief just to be able to say that. I haven't really been in touch with you for all these years and now it's a great feeling to touch you, be touched by you and to experience you again. I had given up you know! I thought that the despair and anger we had was a one-way street. I spent many hours agonizing, then self-pity would start taking over, finally there was anger because I felt helpless. We both know where the anger eventually led.

I wish we had met someone who understood what we were going through back then, but I guess I am to blame. I never gave anyone the chance to love us along. I was always suspicious when anyone tried to get close and it's still my biggest regret. But I didn't know. You know, sometimes after living with a belief for a long time a man can come to expect reactions as second-nature. So even if a man is wrong he might not have the courage or ability to stop his running dialogue. I thought it was just me, looking out for myself by being self protective. God was it a mistake to build myself a cocoon!

Now no problem seems too overwhelming any more. I even look forward to challenges sometimes. I did not see much good in others before but today I can "See". I can smile at my own little mistakes again after being so hard. Life is going to be worth living for us again. Of this I am happily sure and we have an "ally" now to help us along at the rough spots. Stay with me now and don't let me feel sorry for myself no more. I'll provide the strength to you, so you can wipe away the grief of the years.

Bye for the moment

Love,

Julio

Mike...   Letter to myself

Dear Mike,

You know kid that you really screwed up this time. You caused a lot of pain, but that's one thing that you're good at — at causing pain. Hell Mike, at one time you were the master of pain and grief. But now I hear that you changed — Yeah right. Who are you kidding? Not me!! I know you better. I've been with you for all our life and I know that you're not capable of change.... Well, at least, I thought you weren't.

Mike, I'm sorry for all the hatred I've inflicted on you and all the misdirection I've shown you. I didn't mean for us to be here but I'm glad you finally put your foot down and made us change. You know Mike, old buddy, now that the negativity and anger is going out of you maybe we can really make a difference to ourselves and others and maybe show others or they will, I'm sure, see for themselves, how different we truly are.

Mike, we've been through hard times together and most of it was my fault, well, your old selfs fault. Now that you took control of everything I hope you won't let me re-surface and ruin all your good works. I know that now you're in the drivers seat. I wish you took control a long time ago then maybe we wouldn't have been put into this horrible place. Well maybe that's not true. Maybe I put you here to make you stand up to me — to see if you had the guts to change your way of life or if I had you totally under control.

I'm glad you won Mike and I know that NOW we will find the happiness we deserve. I'm sorry for putting you through all this misery but you deserved it for not standing up for yourself and for letting me take control for so long.

Take care,

My new self

Me

P.S. I'm trying to remember that I deserve to like myself, no matter what other people have told me or thought about me in the past. I now understand that I am not what I have done. I am simply who I am.

Releasing Yourself From The Past

Self-forgiveness takes fearlessness. Fearlessness doesn't mean you don't have fear. It means you are willing to acknowledge and work with your fears and move ahead despite them. The ego would prefer to go along with public opinion, see you as unforgivable and unworthy of your own understanding and deepest wisdom. It would prefer to go on with life keeping you "in your place." It doesn't realize your place is not only with the wounded but among the healed as well, not only among the fearful but among the loving and truly powerful. As author Robert Keck writes, "Love is the power and forgiveness is the strategy to release and realize that power." If you open to the lessons that self-forgiveness requires of you, you will discover that, as the famous teacher Joseph Campbell tells us, "where you have stumbled and fallen is where you will find your treasure."

When you start to consider self-forgiveness, if it seems impossible because you have done things that have left behind tremendous destruction, or even damage on a lesser scale, see if you can start by contemplating forgiving yourself in relation to acts of lesser consequence. In truth, however, you are not forgiving the acts, you are forgiving yourself. Author Wayne Muller reminds us that what we are forgiving is not the abuse, the incest, the violence, the pain, the lies, the stealing etc., we are forgiving the people, "the people who could not manage to honor and cherish their own children, their own spouse, themself, and others. We are forgiving their pain, their unskillfulness, their suffering, their desperation."

Take a few minutes to read this statement by Muller a few times and think about it in relation to yourself.

The purpose of self-forgiveness is to shine light on the fears and destructive self-judgments that keep us all captive in the role of our own jailer. In its broadest sense, self-forgiveness is the challenge of being accountable to our highest nature, and learning to know, accept, and love ourselves, regardless of our past. Forgiving yourself is probably the greatest challenge that you (or anyone) will ever meet. It is an enormous challenge for any of us. And it is a particularly painful and hard-won challenge for most inmates.

There is often great resistance to self-forgiveness, for like any significant change, it is a death. It means dying to the habit of keeping ourselves small and unworthy. Yet self-forgiveness is also a great birth. It is inherent in those moments when the compassion, love and glory of the greater Self is born within our direct experience and known beyond old definitions. Regardless of whether we reside inside or outside prison walls, when we forgive, our lives are always transformed.

CHAPTER 13

Forgiveness: A Bold Choice For A Peaceful Heart

To KNOW TRUE freedom, to experience inner power, we all, sooner or later, must make the choice to forgive. As with self-forgiveness, most of us don't make the choice to forgive others because we don't really understand what forgiving means. The result: we don't see forgiveness as a workable option, something that makes good sense and that we can apply to our own relationships. How often do we hear people say, "I could never forgive that person after what he (or she) has done." If you don't really understand forgiveness, and you have been hurt, betrayed, lied to, cheated on, or abused by others, then it is completely understandable that you would think and feel this way.

When I was in my early twenties, I was raped. It was a totally terrifying experience to live through. As days, weeks, months passed, I felt a wide range of emotions — fear, shame, anger, to name but a few. But eventually I came to forgive the man who raped me. First I had to learn what forgiveness meant. What does it mean that I forgave him? The answer to that question is what this chapter is about. And why should I have forgiven after what he did? That question can be answered simply — because I wanted to be happy and free; I didn't want to be his victim forever.

A feature story on forgiveness in *Time* magazine (an issue with the Pope, his attempted assassin, and the words "Why forgive?" on the front cover) read, "The psychological case for forgiveness is overwhelmingly persuasive. Not to forgive is to be imprisoned by the past, by old grievances that do not permit life to proceed with new business. Not to forgive is to yield oneself to another's control. In this sense, forgiveness is a shrewd and a practical strategy for a person or a nation to pursue." We often think of forgiveness as a lofty ideal — but here it is described as "a shrewd and practical strategy" because, as the article points out, "forgiveness frees the forgiver." If we do not forgive, part of us remains stuck in the past, emotionally bound — one half of the handcuffs locked around our wrist and the other half locked around the person we resent.

People often hold the thought that if they forgive someone, they are doing the person they've been angry at a favor — not realizing that forgiveness is, first and foremost, a favor one does for oneself. *Forgiveness is an act of self-interest.* We do it so as not to let our judgments and anger bind us up in somebody else's ignorance, fears, problems. In some cases, we do it so we don't get lost in somebody else's nightmare. If, for example, you were physically abused by an alcoholic parent, you were most likely locked into years of misery. Forgiving that parent can't erase the past. However, it can lead you out of the nightmare that you were pulled into as a child and it can help you to heal from the aftershock now. Forgiving can restore the personal power that you were robbed of.

Although our egos work to convince us that if we forgive we will be weakened, true forgiveness is actually what strengthens us. In a place that can be as dark and negative as prison, forgiveness looks like an unlikely tool for survival. But in fact that is just what it is.

Where To Start

If you feel a lot of anger toward others, or it's been a while since you read the chapter on anger, I recommend that you start by reviewing that chapter. The initial steps in the process of forgiving begin with honestly and constructively dealing with your anger. If you haven't been "practicing forgiveness on neutral territory", I also encourage you to review chapter seven. The concepts in that chapter are the foundation for forgiving anyone, regardless of the circumstances.

If there are certain people that you're not ready or willing to consider forgiving, as you read through this chapter consider forgiving people towards whom you feel minor anger, judgment, and irritation. Each inner gesture of forgiveness we make is like putting down some bricks and walking on less burdened. Each releases you from the hold that another's actions or attitudes have over you. Each gesture allows you to move forward feeling better about yourself and about life.

In an earlier chapter, I used the image of life being like a stone-mill: the people and experiences we encounter either grind us down or polish us up, depending on the way we relate to them. When we hold on to anger and resentment toward others, without question, we are ground down. When we forgive, without question, we are polished up. We lift ourselves out of a limited way of thinking. We see the bigger picture, release ourselves, and are freed.

What Forgiveness Is Not

A limited or wrong understanding of what it means to forgive can easily, and understandably, close the door on the possibility of forgiving others. As we did in the last chapter, let's begin by clearing up some misconceptions about forgiving by looking first at what forgiveness is not.

Forgiveness *is not* pretending, ignoring your true feelings, and acting like everything is just fine when it isn't. Genuine forgiveness cannot be offered if anger and resentment lie below the surface, ignored or denied. Acting like we've forgiven when we're still angry or resentful is like putting whipped cream on top of garbage. It may look good on the surface, but underneath something is rotting. Sometimes people make choices in the name of "forgiveness," when what is occurring isn't forgiveness at all.

To forgive *is not* to condone negative, hurtful and insensitive behavior. By forgiving you are not saying that what a person did is okay or acceptable. Abuse, violence, betrayal, dishonesty are not okay. Forgiveness doesn't mean you approve or support the behavior that has caused you pain. And it does not mean that you should hesitate to take action to change a situation or protect yourself. You may decide to take firm and dramatic action, like leaving a relationship, divorce, staying away from someone, filing a restraining order or other legal action. These actions may be called for or even required to prevent a certain behavior from happening again. Yet, even though a person has acted in a totally unacceptable way, even if you need to keep your distance, it is possible to forgive the person who has acted in these ways.

Forgiveness, as was just pointed out, does *not* mean you will or must act in a particular way. Your behaviors may change if you forgive someone; but they won't *necessarily* change. You can forgive an old friend from whom you've been estranged and not choose to call them up or suggest that they visit again — unless you really want to. Forgiving someone doesn't mean you have to tell them "I forgive you," unless you want to. You can forgive a fellow inmate and not want to hang around with her or him.

I once heard a story of a meditation teacher who travels throughout the U.S. and Europe leading meditation retreats on a certain aspect of the Buddhist teachings called "loving-kindness." She teaches people various ways to cultivate the spirit of loving-kindness in their daily life. On her way to visit with a teacher in India, she was confronted by a man who tried to push her down and steal her luggage. Feeling frightened and angry, she started shoving back. After a minute or so, she was able to push him off and keep her luggage safe.

As she traveled on, she was flooded with hostile and angry feelings. Anyone would consider these reasonable feelings after what she had just gone through. But since her life was devoted to teaching about loving-kindness, she was taken aback that these feelings were so strong in her. When she finally arrived at the home of her teacher, she told him about what had happened and about how angry and hostile she felt. She asked if he could advise her as to how she might have dealt with the situation differently. Her teacher asked if she had an umbrella available at the time of the incident. When she told him that she did, he said "then you should have taken that umbrella and hit that man — with all the loving-kindness in your heart."

I'm not advocating hitting people *no matter* what is in your heart. Rather I suggest again that forgiveness isn't so much about what you do, as it is about the spirit in which you do it.

Forgiveness *is not* forgetting. Sometimes people say, "If I forgive then I'll forget." Yet, in truth, unless an experience is so traumatic that you have repressed it (as often happens in cases of severe childhood abuse), you don't usually forget the more painful or anger-provoking experiences you encounter. When you forgive, you don't forget. Instead, the painful and/or angry emotional charge diminishes or even ceases. You can see a person who has hurt you, remember what they have done, but not get triggered into anger once again. (Or, you get triggered, but the anger doesn't last as long.)

Forgiveness and Setting Limits

The fact that "forgiveness does not mean that you necessarily act in a particular way" is so important that I want to speak to the issue further before going on.

If you forgive someone, it does not mean that you should then trust the person you have forgiven if you sense that the person is not trustworthy. To do so is just being naive. It does not mean being passive or staying in a relationship that is abusive. If you are willing to allow unacceptable behavior again and again in the name of "forgiveness," rather than truly forgiving, you are using "forgiveness" as an excuse for not assuming responsibility for taking care of yourself and making changes that are needed. This is not forgiveness. *This is avoidance.* This dynamic often plays itself out in abusive relationships, whether they be with a co-worker, friend, mate, or anyone else.

In any situation where you are confronted with difficulty you must get clear about what *is* acceptable to you and what *is not* acceptable to you. For example, in a relationship with a mate, it might be acceptable to you if they don't visit very often, even though you would prefer that they did. But it may be unacceptable to you for them to cheat in the relationship. Once you're clear as to what is acceptable or unacceptable, you can set limits and take action whenever possible if the things you consider truly unacceptable keep re-occurring.

If, in your personal relationships, you repeatedly find yourself in a situation that you know is unacceptable or destructive, yet you can't seem to stop it, deal with it effectively, or break away, *get help*. The underlying emotional issues that often tie a person to unhealthy situations can be difficult, if not almost impossible, to see and change without the help of an objective person. A counselor or a support group (like AA, Al Anon, or other 12-step programs) may be needed to help you to break out of a cycle of abuse and work an issue through.

You may encounter situations in prison that are totally unacceptable and to make matters worse, there may be no immediate recourse or help. You may be treated abusively by other inmates or officers and be denied help and protection, not get medication when you need it, be denied some basic right. Of course you will get angry at times like these. But even in these situations, be aware and try as much as possible to use your anger and not get used by it. Do everything you can to change the situation, but don't let yourself get so lost in your anger that you get eaten alive by it — becoming a victim of your own inner life as well.

Don't hand over the power you have to go deep within yourSelf to find an inner place of peace. At times like these meditation, relaxation, and/or prayer are essential. Do everything you can to change a situation while reflecting from time to time on the seed thought in chapter nine: Consider the possibility that "within me is a peacefulness that cannot be disturbed". And then reflect on the seed thought in chapter five: "I do not have to be a (total) victim of the world I see."

What Forgiveness Is

We've looked at the underlying concepts of forgiveness in the preceding chapters. I'll review some of these concepts here, expand on them, share a story that illustrates some important points, and then give an example of how forgiveness could be applied in a situation you might confront everyday.

When you get angry or resentful toward someone, it is highly unlikely that the person who evokes your anger is coming from their true Self. It is unlikely that you would get angry at someone who is being sensitive, caring, responsive, and loving. In all likelihood they are coming from one of their sub-personalities — the controller, the manipulator, insensitive, tuned-out, the abuser. Their behavior is likely to evoke fear and judgment in you. It may be their "manipulative" sub-personality evoking the "angry" or "judgmental" sub-personality in you. Then you have a dynamic that looks like this:

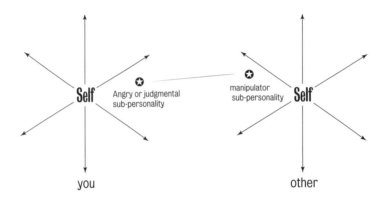

One sub-personality relating to another sub-personality. As I often point out, many marriages stay stuck out in this dynamic for years — one sub-personality relating to another. So how do you break out of this dynamic? Forgiveness is the key.

Forgiveness *is* a choice and decision to see beyond the reactive judgments of our ego. It is the willingness to recognize that a person's insensitive or negative behavior is an expression of his or her separation from Self. It is their constriction and fear that motivates negative behavior. Even though it is not obvious to the unforgiving eye, underlying most negative or insensitive behavior is a call for respect, help, acknowledgment, emotional safety, and love. (Most often this call for respect and safety was not answered in childhood.) It takes considerable insight to see this dynamic because we are so conditioned to see the other person as an idiot or a jerk instead of as someone who is constricted, insecure, or afraid and calling out for love or attention.

The idea of seeing all anger and negative or insensitive behavior as a call for acknowledgment, respect, help, emotional safety, and love is likely a radical departure from the way we have learned to perceive and respond to others. A wonderful illustration of one person's choice to see in this way is described in this true story by Terry Dobson entitled *A Kind Word Turneth Away Wrath.*

A turning point in my life came one day on a train in the suburbs of Tokyo. It was the middle of a calm spring afternoon, and the car was comparatively empty — a few housewives out shopping with their kids in tow, some old folks, a couple of bartenders on their day off poring over the racing form. The rickety old car clacked monotonously over the rails as I gazed absently out at the drab houses and dusty hedgerows.

At one sleepy little station, the doors opened and the drowsy afternoon was shattered by a man yelling at the top of his lungs. A string of loud, violent swears filled the air. Just as the doors closed, the man, still yelling, stumbled into our car. He was a big man, a drunk and exceedingly dirty Japanese laborer. His eyes were a bloodshot, neon red, and his face was filled with hatred and rage. Screaming unintelligibly, he swung at the first person he saw — a woman holding a baby. The blow glanced off her shoulder, but sent her spinning across the car into the laps of an elderly couple. It was a miracle that the baby was unharmed. The couple jumped up and scampered towards the other end of the car. The laborer aimed a kick at the retreating back of the aged grandmother. "YOU OLD WHORE," he bellowed, "I'LL KICK YOUR ASS!" He missed, and the old lady scuttled safely beyond his reach. Beside himself with rage, the drunk grabbed the metal pole in the center of the car and tried to wrench it out of its fixture. I could see one of his hands was cut and bleeding. The train rattled on, the passengers frozen with fear. I stood up.

I was still young, back then, and in pretty good shape. I stood six feet, weighed 225, and had been putting in a solid eight hours of Aikido training every day for the past three years. I was totally absorbed in Aikido. I couldn't practice enough. I particularly enjoyed the harder workouts. I thought I was tough. Trouble was, my skill was yet untried in actual combat. We were strictly enjoined from using Aikido techniques in public, unless absolute necessity demanded the protection of other people. My teacher, the Founder of

Aikido, taught us every morning that Aikido was non-violent. "Aikido," he would say over and over, "is the art of reconciliation. To use it to enhance one's ego, to dominate other people, is to betray totally the purpose for which it is practiced. Our mission is to resolve conflict, not to generate it." I listened to his words, of course, and even went so far as to cross the street a few times to avoid groups of lounging street punks who might have provided a jolly brawl in which I might test my proficiency. In my daydreams, however, I longed for a legitimate situation where I could defend the innocent by wasting the guilty. Such a scene had now arisen. I was overjoyed. My prayers had been answered. I thought to myself, this slob, this animal, is drunk and mean and violent. He's a threat to the public order, and he'll hurt somebody if I don't take him out. The need is real. My ethical light is green."

Seeing me stand up, the drunk shot me a look of bleary inspection. "AHA!" he roared, "A HAIRY FOREIGN TWERP NEEDS A LESSON IN JAPANESE MANNERS!" I held onto the commuter strap overhead, seemingly off-balance.

I gave him a slow, insolent look of contemptuous dismissal. It burned into his sodden brain like an ember in wet sand. I'd take this turkey apart. He was big and mean, but he was drunk. I was big, but I was trained and cold sober. "YOU WANT A LESSON, ASS?" he bellowed. Saying nothing, I looked coolly back at him. He gathered himself for his big rush at me. He'd never know what hit him.

A split-second before he moved, somebody else shouted, "HEY!" It was loud, ear-splitting almost, but I remember it had a strangely joyous, lilting quality to it — as though you and a friend had been searching diligently for something, and he had suddenly stumbled upon it.

I wheeled to my left, the drunk spun to his right. We both stared down at this little old man. He must have been well into his seventies, this tiny gentleman, immaculate in his kimono. He took no notice of me, but beamed delightedly at the laborer, as though he had a most important, most welcome secret to share.

"C'mere," the old man said in an easy vernacular, beckoning to the drunk, "C'mere and talk with me." He waved his hand lightly, and the big man followed as if on a string. The drunk was confused, but still belligerent. He planted his feet in front of the little old man, and towered threateningly over him. "WHAT THE FUCK DO YOU WANT, YOU OLD FART?" he roared above the clacking wheels. The drunk now had his back to me. I watched his elbows, half-cocked as though ready to punch. If they moved so much as a millimeter, I'd drop him in his tracks.

The old man continued to beam at the laborer. There was not a trace of fear or resentment about him. "What you been drinkin'?" he asked lightly, his eyes sparkling with interest.

"I BEEN DRINKIN' SAKE, GOD DAMN YOUR SCUMMY OLD EYES," the laborer declared loudly, "AND WHAT BUSINESS IS IT OF YOURS?"

"Oh, that's wonderful," the old man said with delight, "absolutely wonderful! You see, I just love sake. Every night me and my wife (she's 76, you know) we warm up a little bottle of sake, and we take it out into the garden and we sit on the old bench that my grandfather's student made for him. We watch the sun go down, and we look to see how our tree is doing. My great-grandfather planted that tree, you know, and we worry about whether it will recover from those ice-storms we had last winter. Persimmons do not do well after ice-storms, although I must say ours had done rather better than I expected, especially when you consider the poor quality of soil. But, anyway, we take our little jug of sake and go out and enjoy the evening by our tree. Even when it rains!" He beamed up at the laborer, his eyes twinkling, happy to share the wonderful information.

As he struggled to follow the intricacies of the old man's conversation, the drunk's face began to soften. His fists slowly unclenched. "Yeah," he said when the old man finished, "I love sake too..." His voice trailed off.

"Yes," said the old man, smiling, "and I'm sure you have a wonderful wife."

"No," replied the laborer, shaking his head sadly, "I don't got no wife." He hung his head, and swayed silently with the motion of the train. And then, with surprising gentleness, the big man began to sob. "I don't got no wife," he moaned rhythmically, "I don't got no home, I don't got no clothes, I don't got no tools, I don't got no money, and now I don't got no place to sleep. I'm so ashamed of myself." Tears rolled down the big man's checks, a spasm of pure despair rippled through his body. Up above the baggage rack, a 4-color ad trumpeted the virtues of suburban luxury living. The irony was almost too much to bear. And all of a sudden I felt ashamed. I felt more dirty in my clean clothes and my make-this-world-safe-for-democracy righteousness than that laborer would ever be.

"My, my," the old man clucked sympathetically, although his general delight appeared undiminished, "that is a very difficult predicament, indeed. Why don't you sit down here and tell me about it?"

Just then, the train arrived at my stop. The platform was packed, and the crowd surged into the car as soon as the doors opened. Maneuvering my way out, I turned my head for one last look. The laborer sprawled like a sack on the seat, his head in the old man's lap. The gentleman was looking down at him kindly, a beatific mixture of delight and compassion beaming from his eyes, one hand softly stroking the filthy, matted head.

As the train pulled away from the station, I sat on a bench and tried to re-live the experience. I saw that what I had been prepared to accomplish with bone and muscle had been accomplished with a smile and a few kind words. I recognized that I had seen Aikido used in action, and that the essence of it was reconciliation, as the Founder had said. I felt dumb and brutal and gross. I knew I would have to practice with an entirely different spirit. And I know it would be a long time before I could speak with knowledge about Aikido or the resolution of conflict.

Terry's story brings home the basic truth that people don't vic-
timize, intimidate or threaten others or try to control others unless
they feel out of control, helpless, and powerless themselves. Realizing the psychological dynamics underlying aggressive behavior
doesn't mean that you or I should respond the way the elder gentleman in Dobson's story chose to. In all honesty, if I had been on the
train and was able to recognize the laborer's pain and plea for help,
I probably still would not have asked him to sit next to me or tried
to carry on a conversation with him. I would probably have looked
for the nearest available exit. Again, forgiveness is not about what
we *do*, it is about the way we *perceive* people and circumstances. My
ability to forgive would have totally influenced whether I left the
train feeling anger and hatred or compassion; whether I would have
wanted to see this man hurt or helped; whether my heart would
have been closed or open to him.

Forgiveness teaches us that under behavior that appears heartless
there is a heart; beyond actions that do not have any redeemable
value there is a soul of value — even though, at a personality level,
some may be so constricted and fearful as to be starkly disconnected
from these realities. Forgiveness is an act of true seeing.

Forgiveness implies a willingness to accept responsibility for our
perceptions, realizing that our perceptions are a *choice* and not an
objective fact. Do you see just a jerk in front of you or do you see
someone who is wounded and insecure? In place of the angry
woman or man you saw attacking you an hour ago, you may now see
a frustrated and scared little girl or boy. Again, it is most often the
wounded or frightened child in another who is responsible for their
lack of caring or mature judgment. As you see this you gain the clarity to not personally take offense because of another's fears,
insecurities, and woundedness.

Remember, what we are forgiving is not the act — not the violence, or neglect, or insensitivity — we are forgiving the people. We
are forgiving their ignorance, their suffering, their confusion.

When you have the clarity and insight to see beyond outer appearances to the deeper motivation for a persons behavior, you prevent another's ignorant or fear-based reactions from necessarily leaving you feeling angry and defensive. And as you change your perceptions, your emotional reactions change as well.

Keep in mind that regardless of your current relationship with the people who originally provoked your anger — whether it was an inmate, a parent, a boyfriend, girlfriend, spouse, correctional officer, friend, your child, or whomever — holding on to your anger is a *choice* you make. You might consider your choice in the light of the following: holding on to anger and resentment is like holding on to a burning ember with the intention of throwing it at another, all the while burning yourself.

THROUGHOUT YOUR DAY CONSIDER:

Today I will see all anger, (insensitivity, irritability, hostility, "stupid" behavior, etc.) as a call for acknowledgment, respect, emotional safety, help, and love.

Putting It into Practice

Let's look at an actual scenario of how you might put forgiveness into practice.

Imagine that a person you share a cell with has recently become more controlling, demanding, and difficult to deal with. This person isn't someone who is out of control or totally unreasonable. You don't fear that he (or she) is going to seriously hurt you because you don't do what he asks, but he is definitely disrespectful and selfish at times. Since there hasn't been any reason to believe that you are in any physical danger — although, it feels like a physical encounter is just a push away — your request for another cell-mate won't get considered for a few months. You find your anger toward this person consuming a lot of your emotional energy, and you find more and more images of hurting this person filling your mind. Everytime he "tells" you to do something or puts you down, you want to punch him out. Instead, you either ignore him while boiling inside or you hit back with some choice words. Then things quiet down for a while, but before long a similar scene gets played out again.

One alternative is that you could stay stuck in this dynamic — your cell-mate's controlling, demeaning sub-personality triggering your angry and judgmental sub-personality. Every time a new incident occurs, any chance at feeling okay is destroyed. You find yourself increasingly annoyed. Your emotional state is clearly at the mercy of your cell-mate's behavior.

Now imagine that you are introduced to the concept of forgiveness as it is presented here. What would it mean to actually put forgiveness into practice in this situation?

First, you would have to *decide* to practice forgiveness. You would have to decide to bring a new awareness to the situation and see the whole drama differently. To forgive your cell-mate would mean you are willing to intercept an automatic way of relating to him.

It is a bold choice to step out of familiar ways of operating. The anger might be giving you a feeling of power, or it may feel like a protection in this situation. But it is important to remember that by always using anger as a source of strength or protection, you deny yourself the opportunity of knowing what genuine strength is. As a stance, anger always re-establishes your sense of powerlessness and fear because you unconsciously relinquish the power you have to the person with whom you are angry.

Even though up until now you have seen your cell-mate as nothing more than a _____ (fill in the blank), forgiving means that you decide to see more to him than this. You decide to look beyond his outer behavior for now and remember that all his insensitive, abusive, negative behavior is a sign that he is lost — separate from who he truly is. You see your cell-mate's fear, insecurity, and woundedness. And you take it even one step further to see the fear as a call for help, acknowledgment, emotional safety, respect, and love that was probably never answered as his controlling and demanding sub-personalities formed.

You see that there is more to your cell-mate than meets the eye. Forgiveness requires affirming his wholeness regardless of what fragment you see. You *decide* that even though you definitely can't see any light in this person with your physical eyes, you are going to assume that there is a wise, reasonable, fundamentally good person inside him. You are willing to See the light as well as the lampshade. You see this not from the vantage point of a "superior" or "judging" sub-personality but from the vantage point of the peace, clarity, and understanding of the Self.

Again, forgiving your cell-mate doesn't mean you will act in a particular way. Yet, by forgiving you are most apt to act in a way that doesn't escalate fear and hostility. Forgiving your cell-mate doesn't mean that you will avoid communicating directly about how you feel and what you think about what is happening; it doesn't imply that you will hesitate to call this person on his acts and the issues at hand. But it does means that you are willing to see beyond the act and relate to him about these issues from your wise, centered, clear Self to his Self.

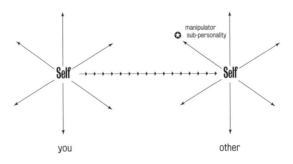

The happiest scenario is that your cell-mate senses that you are non-aggressive and reasonable. He senses that there is something different in where you are coming from — and even though you may call a spade-a-spade, he is able to hear you. You tell your cell-mate how you see the situation — but without condemning him. Not feeling so judged, he lets go of the act, lets down defenses, and is "real". He responds to you from his Self. This Self to Self communication is what solid relationships and true friendships are made of. No relationship ever stays in this place all the time, but with the *intent* to be aware and forgiving, we have more and more moments of relating from this clear and sane perspective.

Another scenario is that you come from your Self, and with greater and greater consistency, day after day, you try to see the bigger picture and relate to the Self in your cell-mate. You deal with the situations as clearly and reasonably as you did in the last scenario. But you find that this person is so lost in habitual fear-based sub-personalities that he keeps reacting in the same old way — hostile, defensive, and shut down. So what do you do then?

On an inner level, there is only one option if you want to be emotionally free, strong, and reasonably peaceful, not living as the angry victim of your cell-mate. This, of course, is to continue forgiving. Every moment of choosing to relate to the Self of this person is a moment in which you are strengthening your identification with your own Self. Even if the circumstances remain very difficult, your new awareness and insight, heightened objectivity, and detachment will allow you to step out of being the emotional victim of this person and situation for more and more moments of your day.

If you are dealing with an ongoing tense situation it can be very difficult to remember to forgive. Your ego will naturally try to pull you into the conflict and justify any and every negative reaction. It is natural and easy to get pulled into negative and fear-ful reactions when we deal with people who are negative and fear-ful. If you are

dealing with a person who really challenges your peace of mind —
and clearly the prison environment potentially poses this challenge
all the time — a daily practice of meditation, exercise, relaxation,
prayer, or other inner work is invaluable and necessary to help you
become and stay as clear and centered as possible. As you work at
staying centered, you may even find yourself experiencing compassion for the sure misery that your cell-mate experiences (whether he
or she acknowledges it or not).

> AS YOU GO THROUGH YOUR DAY, AFFIRM
> ### I am determined to See.

Forgiveness releases you from weaving complex scenarios of
anger, guilt, blame and justification. It challenges you to deal with
the real issues, to see fear for what it is and to develop clarity, establish boundaries, take explicit action when it is called for — all
while not losing touch with yourSelf.

In any ongoing relationship, whether with a cell-mate, spouse,
guard, or anyone else who triggers your judgments and anger, forgiveness is *never* a one-time event. You may genuinely See and forgive in one moment, and ten minutes later you may be angry again.
Forgiveness, like any state of mind or heart, doesn't last in time. You
only have this moment and now this moment and now this moment.
Each time you notice yourself forgetting, remind yourself that in
each moment of awareness, you can choose a wiser, more insightful
way of seeing the situation. You can bring a new understanding to
it. There is an expression that, "understanding all *is* forgiving all."

Forgiveness teaches us that we can disagree with someone without having to keep our hearts closed and remain angry. Forgiveness
takes us beyond the fears and survival mechanisms of our conditioning to a certain boldness of vision that allows for a new realm of

choice and freedom where we can put more and more of our struggles to rest. It guides us to where peace is not a stranger. It empowers us to know our true strength.

When Verbal Communication Is Part of Forgiveness

In many circumstances words never need to be exchanged for forgiveness to be real and complete for us. Yet in any ongoing relationship where mutual cooperation is called for (whether this is with a intimate partner or cell-mate or co-worker) the ability to communicate clearly and honestly is essential for nurturing an atmosphere of forgiveness. Sometimes it is necessary to complete a matter. Sometimes it is necessary to keep intimacy intact. In a close ongoing relationship, if there are unresolved issues, and there is no real communication, there will inevitably be anger, resentment, frustration, and a lot of second guessing about what the other person is thinking and feeling.

In order to verbally communicate in a way that nurtures forgiveness it is necessary to:

1. be aware of what the real issues are for you;

2. be in touch with the truth of how you feel;

3. decide what thoughts and feelings would be useful to share;

4. articulate these thoughts and feelings in as clear and non-blaming way as possible;

5. share your truths from your Self to the Self of the person you are communicating with.

My friend Jake was frequently furious with his wife for not taking more responsibility around the house. When he looked closely at what was really going on for him and what he was feeling under the obvious anger, he discovered a profound sense of disappointment and sadness that his marriage was not the supportive partnership he once thought it would be. As a result of this new awareness, the next time he got angry at his wife, rather than being hostile he shared his heartfelt disappointment and sadness with her. Instead of his wife's usual counter accusations for feeling judged and misunderstood, she listened, felt his disappointment, and responded with a sincere willingness to work as more of a team.

If Jake hadn't acknowledged the pain and disappointment under his anger and taken the risk to communicate these feelings to his wife in a non-blaming way, he and his wife would probably still be living in their own emotionally isolated worlds. True communication always inspires connection rather than separation.

EXERCISE

Getting Clear

The following phrases are designed to help you get clear about what you are feeling and what the real issues are in a relationship where you are angry or upset. Even if you don't or can't actually speak with the person you choose, completing the following will help you understand your circumstances and yourself better — and self-understanding always leads to greater freedom.

As you complete the following sentences, allow yourself to be open to whatever thoughts or feelings that arise. It can be very useful to actually write your responses and reflect on them after you have completed the writing.

Before you do the exercise, close your eyes and take a few letting go breaths. Then think of a situation in your life where you often feel angry or upset. (You can use this exercise in relation to anyone.) Keeping this person and situation in mind, complete the following sentences.

The issue is _____.
The issue is _____.
The real issue is _____.
The real issue is _____.

The real issue is _____.
The issue is really _____.

Continue using these phrases and filling in the blanks, until you have exhausted your responses. Repetition will help you get at what the real issue is. For example my friend Jake may have hit on five or six other issues before he got to his disappointment about his marriage not being an the real partnership he wanted.

In relation to this person or situation, what I'm feeling is

_____.
What I'm feeling is _____.
What I'm really feeling is _____.
What I'm also feeling is _____.
I also feel _____.
And under that feeling is _____.
And under that feeling is _____.
And under that feeling is _____.

Breathe. Look inward and complete the following:
What I'm afraid of is _____.
What I fear is _____.
What I'm afraid of is_____.
What scares me is _____.
What really scares me is _____.
What I'm really afraid of is _____.
Be gentle and compassionate with yourself.

In order to step out of ineffective patterns of relating, as mentioned before, it is also important to reflect on what is acceptable and unacceptable for you in the relationship. Now that you know what you are feeling, think about what is acceptable and unacceptable for you in this relationship.

Continuing to reflect on the relationship or situation from above, complete the following sentences:

What is unacceptable to me is _____.

What is unacceptable to me is _____.

What I can't handle is _____.

What I can't handle is_____.

I can't handle it because _____.

I can't handle it because _____.

What I need to do, (if anything,) to make it acceptable is _____.

What I need to do to make it acceptable is _____.

What needs to change to make this acceptable is _____.

Even if you are dealing with the same relationship, your responses to these sentence completions may change from time to time. Allow for change and flexibility when it is the truth of your experience.

It may be painful to acknowledge the truth but it is an essential step toward forgiveness.

Forgiving Parents: An Essential Step In Emotional Healing

One's parents are often among the most difficult people to forgive. They are often the first significant people to hurt us. And what's worse, they do so at a time when we are truly helpless, vulnerable, and dependent.

Yet, forgiving one's parents is an essential component of emotional healing. And like any step in emotional healing, one has to be ready and willing. If you feel angry at your parent(s) and don't feel like you want to forgive them, most importantly, be gentle with yourself. Respect your feelings. Yet even if you feel this way, I encourage you to read this section over — perhaps you will find a few ways of thinking about them and your relationship that will be healing and helpful. If you feel like you have nothing to forgive your parents for, I encourage you to read on anyway.

If you were mistreated, abused, or abandoned by your mother or father — if you were anything less than loved and cared for by these people whom you needed and counted on most — then, in all likelihood, you carry some anger, grief, and disappointment from not having had some of your basic needs met. As you consider the possibility of forgiving your parents you may think, "But I have a right to be angry after what my father did." "I have a right to be angry after the way my mother treated me." And indeed, you absolutely *do* have a right to be angry! Again, it is important to feel the anger if it is how you feel. As you know, the first step in healing is acknowledging and dealing with your present feelings.

* * *

When the umbilical cord that connects us to our mother is cut at birth, physically we become our own separate person. As we move into adulthood if we feel angry and resentful toward our parents, we remain connected by another cord — a psychic cord made up of anger, resentment, guilt, shame, and/or blame — despite the illusion of separation and autonomy. If that cord remains connected, a part of us never gets to grow up. Our emotional and spiritual growth becomes stunted. As with all resentment, we are held an emotional hostage to the past.

Perhaps your anger isn't from your childhood, but from present day circumstances. Perhaps your parents aren't emotionally supportive or they don't try to contact you, write, or visit. Perhaps you feel abandoned by them now that you are incarcerated. Whatever the circumstances, forgiving your parents is part of the process of becoming a healthy and powerful man or woman.

Some people fear forgiving their parents because they believe that by forgiving they will once again make themselves vulnerable, open to being taken advantage of and hurt. Forgiving ones' parents, like forgiving anyone else, doesn't mean that you necessarily hesitate to call them on what is going on or what has happened in the past. It also doesn't mean that you have to have an active relationship with them if it doesn't feel like it is in your best interest at this time. If, for instance, one of your parents is emotionally abusive and/or an active addict, it may be an act of self-love to stay away from that parent, especially if you need some time to deal with your own feelings and gain clarity and strength. You can forgive them and still set clear, non-negotiable boundaries. However you choose to act, forgiving them will empower you to no longer take their negative, insensitive, or abusive behavior so personally — even though as a child there was no way to take their behavior but personally.

Although your parents may be older than you in the number of years they have lived, they may be emotionally wounded children themselves. They might be forty, fifty, or eighty years old on the outside, but wounded six year olds on the inside. Obviously a wounded six year old couldn't give you the love, respect, and safety you needed and deserved.

In order to forgive your parents and experience the healing that comes with that process, you must be willing to consider that given their circumstances, your parents did and are doing the best they can. A father who was abandoned might find it hard work to make a full, open connection with you. A mother raised by rageful parents, might have to work hard at being a patient and gentle parent. Whether your parents are ready, willing or able to do this work is not up to you. We can only forgive our parents when we begin to give up unrealistic expectations that they will suddenly be who we want them to be.

PAUSE AND REFLECT

Take a few deep relaxing breaths. Now see your mother as a young child. Imagine her in her childhood. Imagine what shaped her personality. Was she emotionally nurtured and supported by her parents? Were her feelings honored and validated or dismissed or treated with disrespect? What fears and successes shaped her sense of security and self-love? Did her parents serve as models of what a loving parent could be?

Now imagine your father as a little boy. Repeat this exercise keeping your father in mind. Imagine what it was like to grow up in his shoes.

Now consider:

Are you willing to entertain the possibility that given the truth of your parents own childhood experiences and their current degree of emotional and spiritual maturity, they have done and are doing the very best that they can?

In order to forgive, you have to be willing to stop looking to your parents for what they may not be capable of giving at this time. By doing this, you step out of the family drama and, with greater compassion, see them as the wounded people they may be.

Letting Go of Expectations

Again, part of forgiving your parents requires letting go of the expectations that demand what they cannot give. You may want your parents to be different, you may actively support them in changing, but in order to forgive and have peace of mind, you have to let go of any attachment to your parents being a certain way. If you demand — even at a subtle level— from your parents what they may not be capable of giving you at this time, you will keep anger, resentment and guilt alive for all involved.

Think of something you want from your mother. It might be love, acceptance, affection, approval, money. In your imagination, see yourself with your mother. Remember to breathe. Now tell her what you want from her. Say, "Mother (or whatever you call her), what I want from you is_____ and _____ .

List as many things as you need to until you feel complete. Take a deep breath. Feel the wholeness within your own being. Then say to her "Mom (or whatever you call her), I no longer hold you responsible for giving me _____ (whatever you listed before).

Now imagine you are with your father and repeat this exercise.

Who's Taking Care of You?

The job of emotionally taking care of yourself must shift from your parents to yourself. It is up to you to proceed with your life, making the choices that nurture and support you. If your parents are alive yet unable to really show up for you emotionally, what you had needed, wanted, and expected them to give you, you will need to seek from others, yourSelf, and your spiritual life.

Again (and again), understanding that your parents may have done the best they could, doesn't mean that you condone their behavior or that you should hesitate to address the issues or feelings that remain unresolved — if you feel it would be useful to do so. Make sure, however, that if you address the issues you do not expect that your parents will necessarily change. Even if your communication falls on deaf or resistant ears, you will know that you have tried to open communication and heal the relationship.

There may come a time when you have to evaluate how long to persist with sharing the truth of your experience if it appears to be falling on deaf ears. It is important to watch your own level of frustration and to give up (at least for now) if you feel consistently worse each time you try to break through. A general rule you might try would be to share your truth once — if it is met with resistance, let it go for now. If the issue comes up again for you, share it again, perhaps in a different way. If a third attempt at communication fails, let it go as best you can. This person is just not ready to hear you yet and perhaps you've done all you can for now. Be willing to let go of the outcome of your interaction. If their reaction evokes more anger and pain, get the support you need or take it upon yourself to deal with the feelings that are evoked. Just your sincere effort to communicate and initiate positive change can result in a feeling of greater freedom and completion for you. At least you will know you have tried your best.

EXERCISE

A Letter of Forgiveness to a Parent

After working with this chapter write a letter of forgiveness to each parent (and/or primary caretaker). Forgiveness doesn't mean ignoring the harm that happened. It starts with facing it — and being willing to have healing occur despite it. Remember, any forgiveness starts with the willingness to acknowledge your true feelings. If all you feel is anger, then express your anger.

* * *

You don't need to send the letter but it will give you an opportunity to get your thoughts and feelings out. Getting the truth out in the open is an important part of the healing process. But if you are going to send the letter, it is important that you pay careful attention to the spirit in which you do your truth-telling in order not to keep a cycle of conflict and anger going. The spirit in which you communicate helps to determine whether a cycle of pain and anger will be continued or interrupted.

The following are letters to parents from participants in the Emotional Awareness class. Ron's father was not alive when he wrote this, but writing a series of letters to his father was an important part of his healing process.

Ron

Dear Dad,

I wrote you an angry letter about a week ago and I thought I'd write another one this morning. I was really sad, hurt and disappointed in you for not having been a father to and for me when I needed one the most. I don't know if you were capable of being a father, and by father I mean being there emotionally, supportive, encouraging, guiding, loving, and all the rest that goes with being a dad. I like to think that you are sad about it as well. I thought something was wrong with me because of your rejection and abandonment. I took it upon myself to blame myself for your terrible inadequacies. I know today that I was a beautiful, loving and lovable little boy deserving of your love and support. I feel kind of pity for you Dad as you had nine beautiful children and you couldn't or wouldn't let us enrich your miserable existence. You didn't even notice. You must have suffered terribly. And we all suffered along with you.

Dad I know the disease of alcoholism took everything from you. You died a very lonely man, embittered by what you thought were all the wrongs... real or imagined... done you. Feeling sorry for you kept my anger, hurt, sadness, confusion and all kinds of other feelings from ever surfacing. I had to get in touch with my anger, disappointment and all the rest. I want to let it all go. I want to make room for love. I don't want to die an embittered old man. I want to die with business finished.

I no longer hold you responsible for giving me love, acceptance, respect. I no longer need you for that Dad. I have me today. I have me! The reason I emphasize "I have me" is I didn't have me before. I drank just like you Dad. I became an alcoholic. I abused women just like you Dad. I abandoned my only child just like you Dad.

Dad I had no role model to become a man. I had no guidance. No one to lead the way. I grew up or rather survived the streets. Dad I have spent my entire life searching for the love, acceptance and validation from other men. I trusted an older man and he took whatever innocence that I had. And then I continued seeing this man who molested me. At least he gave me attention and what I thought was love. I learned to reach out to people in the only way I knew how. I let people use me sexually. I became even more confused, lonely and heart sick. Pretending always pretending to have it all together when in reality I felt afraid, desperate, and lonely. I no longer want to have to give of myself for love and acceptance. I know today I was deserving of your love and acceptance. I know today that I can do for myself and not have to search out people whose only real interest has been to bed me in my confused attempt at getting love and acceptance.

Do you realize how much rage I carried around in myself. Only to unleash it on totally innocent people. Crushing their skulls in and severely brain damaging a third. I have to live with that today. Thank God I am doing something about my rage today. I have addressed my alcoholism, I am sober today. I am no longer running away from life today. I am facing myself and I am learning to reach out and ask for help in healthy ways today. For the first time in my life, I think that I am a loving, lovable fragile human being who has taken a severe beating most of his life. Been a victim most of his life and doesn't want to live my life as a damn victim anymore. And I have the opportunity to free myself from the past. And damnit I want freedom. I want to be happy. I no longer want to live life thinking it is a burden. I want to live life as if it is an adventure. Bringing love and peace to those that I can touch.

Dad, I can be a man today even without your guidance. I feel very sorry Dad that you never had that opportunity. Dad I loved you in spite of yourself. I am working on forgiving you and myself too.

Good Bye Dad

Your Loving Son

Ron

Ray's letter to his mother, who was no longer living at the time he wrote it, confronts her with some hard truths in an open way, while acknowledging her own pain and upbringing.

Ray

Dear Mother,

I've been doing a lot of thinking about you, us, and our lives, in general. I pray that you and Dad are back together now, loving in the after life. Dad missed you so. You were his reason for living even though you were gone.

As I go through life, I realize how you and I are so much alike. It seems that I love and dislike alot of the same things, but what bothers me is that many of your bad habits have rubbed off on me. I remember how you would just explode at me and become so violent, yelling and screaming and carrying on so, over trivial things like me chewing too loud, things that shouldn't have caused such a reaction. Big things didn't seem to bother you, like the flood of 1971. You were such a rock through it. I find that I am the same way and I don't think that I inherited it from you. I think that I learned it all from you and that you learned it from your father. You had such an influence on my life and my actions. I was blind to all of this before but with new awareness and insight that I have gained into myself, I'm beginning to feel like I have never felt, be like I've never been, and love like I've never loved.

Ma, I love you, I hope that you know that. If you don't I'm telling you now, *I LOVE YOU*!!! What is most important for me right here, right now is the fact that I have forgiven you. You may say, "Well what the hell do I have to be forgiven for?" Even though it's painful, maybe I should bring up a few things. Do you remember how angry you would get at me and throw me on the floor and kick me in the ribs? I know you don't because you denied it until the day you died, but I remember being kicked like a dog. Remember telling me that you wish that I was never born? You probably don't. Well, I do. How about the time when I got run over by the car? Ma! I was only 18 months old. What was I doing on the street by myself at that age. I can remember that pain! I remember these things and much more. I think that you can realize now how much these things hurt me and that they affect me even today. It is time to start over with a new slate. I wish that you were here to hear all this, face to face, Self to Self, but you're not, but I can forgive you even though you are gone. Maybe you can hear my heart crying. Maybe you can feel my pain. Ma, I forgive you and please, if you are hurt with all of this confession, forgive me too. I just feel like it all has to be said.

Ma, you probably learned it from your mother and father and they got it from theirs. Love breeds love. Hate breeds hate. Violence breeds violence. Yelling breeds yelling. Giving breeds giving. Do you see what I am trying to say? It's the way that I was brought up that has made me what I am or should I say — was. Ma, I am evolving into a new being. I am finding my true Self, the real Ray, not the one that was created by your influence but the one that was created by God.

Maybe with dialogue we both sort of died but with death comes life and with life can come peace. I pray that now that I have done this, the pain and hurt can be put behind me and a new life can begin. Ma, it has already.

With all my love,

Ray

Ralph's letter to his mother stresses the important idea that healing is possible as he acknowledges that they both did "their best" despite their obvious limitations.

Ralph

Dear Mom,

I'm writing you today to tell you I love you. I want to let you know I have peace in my heart now, and for the first time in my life, "I see you". I see your pain, I feel your hurt! I know now you have always done the best you could for me. I want both of us to stop feeling guilty for a past we had no control over. We have lost most of the last twenty-six years to guilt, resentment, anger and sorrow. I am truly sorry for being so angry and blaming. You see mom, I never knew who to blame at seven. I only knew I wanted to come home with you and couldn't. At seven I didn't know anybody else had any say. To me, you were God and could do anything you wanted — even though it wasn't true. I held onto that pain and rejection without ever even knowing it. Emotionally I stayed seven years old, until now, at 33. I am as sorry for you, as I am for myself. I don't want you to feel guilty anymore. None of this is our fault. We both did "all" we could do, and thought what we did do was for the best. I forgive you ma, but what's more important to me is you forgive yourself. I want you to have peace in your heart, and it can only be found through forgiveness.

Love,

Ralph

As you reflect on your relationships with your parents, you may feel that the person you need to forgive is yourself. Remember this: no matter what you did as a child, no matter how "bad" you were told you were, it is critical for you to remember and accept that none of the abuse was your fault. If you want to heal, you have to remember that you did the best you could have done considering the scope of your awareness and the depth of fear you were experiencing.

Many parents blame their unhappiness on their children. For instance, one of my friends grew up hearing, "If it weren't for you, your father and I would be so happy." Her healing began with forgiving herself, recognizing that she was not responsible for her mother's unhappiness. Her healing continued by feeling angry at her mother and later forgiving her mother for having burdened her with that guilt for so many years.

You may feel that you need to forgive yourself for not having listened to the warnings and advice of your parents as you grew older. You may feel like you failed and disappointed your parents. The past is over now. The issue at hand is learning from your experience — so that you don't fail yourself. If this was the case, whether you send it or not, I encourage you to write a letter asking for forgiveness. Regardless of whether they forgive you or not, the bottom line is learning to accept, like, and love yourself.

Jose

Dear Mom,

I honestly apologize and ask for forgiveness, for all the wrong things I have done. For all the hard times I have put you through, for all the things I was supposed to do and didn't do, for all the things I did to disappoint you, for not listening to your words of wisdom, when now that I think about it, I wouldn't be in the situation I am if I had listened. I hope that you could look in my heart and see that I mean what I'm saying. I love you, always have and always will.

Your son,

Jose

Todd

Dear Mom,

I've always wanted to tell you this but my mind and heart would not allow it. I'm sorry mom that I didn't turn out as you would have wanted me to and that I went in the wrong direction. But I did and

I'm now sorry for all the hurt and pain that I've caused you. I only hope you can forgive me for being so thick-headed and not listening as I should have.

I know that I was wrong. I hope that you will stick by me and help give me strength to continue in my new direction.

Love,

Todd

Healing Your Relationship with Your Parents After They Have Died

If you had a painful relationship with your parents and they died before you had a chance to heal your relationship, you may feel that you've lost your chance to come to peace with them. Considering the options that were obvious to you, forgiving may not have been possible earlier. Remember to be gentle with yourself.

If you had a painful relationship with deceased parents, their deaths may have felt like a welcome relief. You may have thought "the relationship is finally over and I won't have to deal with them anymore." Yet, even after their death, "unfinished business" with them takes its toll on your well-being until it is resolved.

Regardless of how you felt about their death or how you related with them while they were alive, it is possible to heal the relationship now.

Certainly it is still possible for you to forgive them. Your willingness to forgive them only takes you.

It has been my experience that a profound sense of mutual healing is also possible. Toward the end of forgiveness workshops that I give for the general public, I facilitate a "Forgiveness" visualization. Before the visualization begins, participants choose someone toward whom they feel some anger or resentment *and* toward whom they are open to the possibility of forgiving and sharing a healed relationship. In the visualization participants are encouraged to invite the person they have chosen to an imaginary safe place.

When I lead this visualization in a large group, almost without fail, a deceased person (frequently a parent), will come into a few of the participants' awareness. (Sometimes the participant has chosen someone other than a parent and, to their surprise, a deceased parent appears.) In the course of the meeting with this person, forgiveness is often expressed both ways. Through hearing the deceased person talk in this process, the person gains insight into the dead person's side of the experience. The opportunity to empathize with the other's experiences and points of view allows the opportunity to both understand and deal with the hurt. As a result, a deep emotional healing often occurs.

Whether your parents are deceased or alive, if you are willing to open to the possibility of healing your relationship with them, try the forgiveness visualization that follows.

EXERCISE

Forgiveness Visualization

Find a comfortable position, close your eyes, and take some long, deep breaths. As you breathe out, feel the tension releasing from your body and mind. Repeat this several times.

Now imagine that you are in a safe and comfortable place. You may have been there before or you may create such a place in your mind. Notice how this place looks and how peaceful it feels. Feel yourself being comfortable here, calm and relaxed. Breathe in and feel a calm strength within you. Now think of someone for whom you feel some resentment... perhaps a parent or someone else. It could be somebody from the past or someone you see everyday. Picture this person in your mind. Breathe in and feel your own inner strength. As you breathe out, let go of any fear or worry.

Now invite the person you just pictured in your mind into this safe place. Breathe in and feel the wholeness within your own being... And allow yourself to look at this person... And now begin to relate to this person, communicating the thoughts and feelings that until now have been left unsaid. With a willingness and courage allow yourself to share the truth of your experiences....

Now allow yourself to hear as this person shares with you. Listen fully for the words and feelings that may not even be spoken. With openness and patience listen to them. Fully hear what they have to say.... Listen for the truth behind their words.... Let go of any blame and judgments.... Let go of the pride that holds on to resentment.

Breathe in and feel the wholeness within your own being. Allow yourself to look into their eyes. Let go of your fear and see beyond their fear. Let go of the burden of resentment and allow yourself to forgive. Let go of judgments and see with new clarity. Look beyond this person's mistakes and errors and allow yourself to see their wholeness....

Now again look into their eyes and allow the issues that stood between you to grow dim and disappear. Breathe in, and feel your own inner strength. If there is anything else you wish to tell this person, take a few moments to share it now....

Now allow yourself to let go of the past and see this person as if for the first time. In this moment, each of you knowing who the other person really is.... Now, with a sense of freedom, say good-bye and watch as this person leaves....

Now allow yourself to extend this forgiveness to yourself.... Let go of unhealthy guilt or self-blame.... Let go of self-judgment.... Make room for yourself in your own heart... Open your heart to yourself, knowing that you deserve your love. Feel a growing freedom as your heart opens fully to your power to love, to be fully alive....

Get ready to open your eyes.... Feel yourself becoming alert ... And when you are ready, open your eyes and go on with your day.

* * *

The "Forgiveness Visualization" can be used to help heal your relationship with anyone. I encourage you to return to this visualization often as you practice forgiveness with others.

The more you choose a loving awareness, the more consistent, integrated and natural an expression forgiveness becomes. And forgiving always leaves you feeling more peaceful and whole.

Remember, however, that forgiveness doesn't necessarily last in time (especially at first when there has been a lot of judgment and anger in the past). You may feel like you have finally forgiven someone. Then minutes later a remark or memory evokes anger again. Often, the stronger and more healed you become, the more you are able to allow the deeper and more hidden anger to come forth. Remember that forgiveness isn't an achievement as much as it is an ongoing process. *Be gentle with yourself.* The issues that are unresolved with your parents, or in other areas of your life, keep arising *for the purpose of healing.*

As it says in the book, *A Course In Miracles*, "Choose once again. Together you remain prisoners of fear, or leave your house of darkness and walk into the light that forgiveness brings."

Although forgiveness is ultimately crucial for the times we feel angry, if we want to be free, healed and able to move on, it is, in it's broadest sense, a pervasive way of relating to life that is clear, compassionate, and understanding.

THROUGHOUT YOUR DAY CONSIDER:
I am determined to See.

CHAPTER 14

Spiritual Awakening: Finding the Faith that Sustains You

Arnie I saw guys who had been using drugs and who were cold-blooded jerks find God — and you see a miracle. You see them completely change. You see them start to care about others. You think if there was hope for that person, if that person could change, then there's hope for me and you want what they have. You begin to believe and know that there's a greater power directing things because you see that power reveal itself. For me, it's not about reading the bible or going to church. It's about a connection. It's about the way you live your life. It's like there's a bigger plan and your life fits into it.

WE ARE ALL spiritual beings by nature. Just as we grow physically, emotionally, and mentally, we have an in-born drive and need to grow spiritually — and when we do grow spiritually our lives are forever changed in a profoundly positive way. Yet despite this fact, we live in a culture that denies the spiritual. Our gods have become money, outer power, excitement, glamour. But we didn't come here to worship false gods or to limit ourselves to the ego. Each of us has come to discover what it really means to be fully human. As the philosopher Heidegger once wrote, "A person is not a thing or a process but an opening through which the Absolute can manifest."

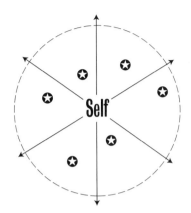

No Boundaries

If you look at the model we have been working with, you see the ego or small selves. You can see that each one has a distinct boundary around it. It is limited and closed off. Now notice when you look at the diagram that the true Self or Spiritual Self at the core of our being has no boundaries. It extends beyond the personality and physical body. It is connected with All That Is.

As you get in touch with the Self, in addition to being more centered, insightful, forgiving, and confident in your ability to meet lifes challenges, you open to the awareness of a Greater Reality. This Greater Reality lets you know that you are never alone, even if in solitary confinement for months or years. (And when I write "you are never alone," I am not referring to the presence of correctional officers or video surveillance!) As the respected religious teacher Paul Tillich so beautifully put it, "...I would like to say to those who feel deeply their hostility toward life: Life accepts you, life loves you as a separated part of itself; life wants to unite you with itself, even when it seems to destroy you."

Every human needs to experience connection with the bigger reality. When life is difficult and we don't sense this connection, we feel lost and alone in the dark — fearful, defeated, on the defensive, or ready to attack. When we are lost in the small selves we feel separate, even though our ever-present spiritual Self knows no boundaries or separation.

Rumi, a great spiritual teacher of the 13th century, shared this passage in his teachings:

> The master said there is one thing in this world which must never be forgotten. If you were to forget everything else, but were not to forget this, there would be no cause to worry, while if you remembered, performed, and attended to everything else, but forgot this one thing, you would in fact have done nothing whatsoever. It is as if a king had sent you to a country to carry out one special, specific task. You go to the country and you perform a hundred other tasks, but if you have not performed the task you were sent for, it is as if you have performed nothing at all. So man has come into the world for a particular task, and that is his purpose. If he doesn't perform it, he will have done nothing.

Throughout the ages spiritual teachers have told us that the purpose of life on earth is to achieve union with our true nature. Teacher Sogyal Rinpoche writes, "The task for which the king has sent us into this strange, dark country is to realize our true nature, our spiritual nature. But how do we search for the spiritual, the soul, God, our inner voice? How do we find these treasures? How do we tap into these transforming and healing powers? There is only one way to do this, and that is to undertake the spiritual journey...."

The spiritual path is not for those who need it (since we all do), but for those who want it. If you want it, you can undertake that journey through commitment and participation in a particular religion, through reading religious, spiritual, or inspirational books, through meditation, prayer, service to others, studying with a spiritual teacher, or through whatever path you may choose or be drawn to. All paths lead to the hidden treasures of love, wholeness, and a sense of peace beyond any peace possible without the spiritual dimension of life. If you dedicate yourself to finding your spiritual nature, you have gone to the land where the king has sent you, and you have accomplished the task for which you were sent.

Religion and Spirituality

When many people think of spirituality, they immediately think of organized religion — the Catholic Church, the Protestant Church, Judaism, Islam, etc. Although organized religions can nurture a deep and profound spiritual life, religion and spirituality are not necessarily the same. Sometimes they lead us to see the same things, but they are often very different. One need not be outwardly religious to be deeply spiritual.

In addressing this issue, therapist, Dr. Naomi Rachel Remen wrote:

A religion is a dogma, a set of beliefs about the spiritual and a set of practices which arise out of those beliefs. There are many religions and they tend to be mutually exclusive. That is, every religion tends to think that it has "dibs" on the spiritual — that it's "The Way". Yet the spiritual is inclusive. It is the deepest sense of belonging and participation. We all participate in the spiritual at all times, whether we know it or not.

There's no place to go to be separated from the spiritual, so perhaps one might say that the spiritual is that realm of human experience which religion attempts to connect us to through dogma and practice. Sometimes it succeeds and sometimes it fails. Religion is a bridge to the spiritual — but the spiritual lies beyond religion. Unfortunately in seeking the spiritual we may become attached to the bridge rather than crossing over it.

Spiritual Growth

Emotional and spiritual healing are intertwined. One supports the other. The work of healing emotional wounds opens the way for a deeply rooted spirituality. When you ignore the emotional work and get involved only with religion or spirituality, there is the potential for ending up with a kind of immature version that is intolerant and that can quickly wear thin when confronted with challenging times. You can end up with a superficial kind of "jail house religion," one that gets left behind when you walk through the gate. If you embrace the light, without embracing the dark (doing some of the emotional work of breaking through denial, pain, anger, or self-hatred), then religion or spirituality can be used as an escape rather than a means for healing. As author Robert Keck writes, "We start discovering the kingdom of heaven by loving, affirming and empowering that part of the universe over which we have responsibility — ourselves." When you do the work of emotional healing as well as nurture your spiritual life, the darkness and light within you can meet and then, like never before, you can experience self-understanding, compassion, and great relief.

Nurturing the Spiritual Life

Although prison may look like a spiritual wasteland, no outer gate, wall or fence can ever keep you from a connection with the spiritual. It is always as close as your breath, as near as your heart.

Even if you haven't put any energy into your spiritual life before, if you are open and willing to put some sincere energy into it now, you open the way for the deepest healing possible. (Your efforts may include things such as participation in religious programs and services, meditation, prayer, reflecting on religious/spiritual/ inspirational writing, or whatever things feel right to you. Spiritual healing leads to a feeling of safety and love that can uplift and sustain you even through the most difficult of circumstances and the darkest of times.

If you lift weights on a regular basis, even if you don't believe that your muscles will develop, they develop anyway. In the same way, even if at first you don't believe that time devoted to prayer, meditation, and inner work will make a difference, you will discover that your life is changed for the better. That is, it will *if* you devote your attention to your spiritual life.

There are many ways to nurture one's spiritual life and each person must find his or her own way. If we are sincere in our search, each of us will find the way(s) that are right for us. Assuming that there is no one way that is *the* way for everyone, some different ways of nurturing a connection with the spiritual dimension of life (and with the highest and best within you) will be offered here.

In order to (hopefully) avoid offending anyone and to avoid writing a long list of names many times, I will refer to whomever/whatever you pray to as "A Higher Power" or "A Greater Reality" — for you that may be God, Jesus, Allah, a saint, the Virgin Mary, the Holy Spirit, or any of many possibilities. As they say in the 12-step programs, this is about "your experience and understanding of a higher power."

Prayer

*Everyone prays in their own language,
and there is no language that God does not understand.*
—Duke Ellington

Like any spiritual practice to which we sincerely give ourselves, prayer can change us in profound ways. Whether the change is a change in circumstance, a new found faith, a miracle of healing, or a more peaceful heart, prayer is powerful medicine for the soul. When we pray, even if we pray alone, we change from individuals isolated and alone in the world to people connected to A Greater Reality.

Prayer gives us a chance, in our own personal way, to ask for help, offer thanks, confess our wrongdoings, and listen to a voice of comfort and encouragement. We give up sole ownership of our life and stop trying to make our way all by ourselves. By praying we invite a higher power in. We allow ourselves to be guided and pointed in the right direction.

There is enormous support for you in the universe! But you have to want it. Invite it. And not walk away if you feel like your knock isn't answered the first time you call. Keep knocking. Some-One is home!

To really know the power of prayer, you can't do it once in a great while and forget about for the rest of the time. "A single meditation, prayer, or talk with God is a great first step, but," as prison educator, Bo Lozoff writes, "it's like reading only page one of a great book and then saying, 'Yep, that's great,' and putting it away on the shelf. We must remind ourselves of what we believe in, we must find ways to deepen and strengthen those beliefs, we must see how they hold up under pressure. We must make spiritual practice part of our ordinary life experiences throughout each day."

There are many ways of praying from various traditions. Here are some I find especially effective in building spiritual muscle and connecting us to the source.

Asking: The turning point in any healing for alcoholics or addicts is admitting their illness, admitting that they can't heal alone, and asking for help. Help comes when we sincerely ask. It takes a certain humility and courage to ask—really ask—for help. To ask means we are really willing to have our life changed, really willing to have a change of heart.

Of course you can ask for anything you want in prayer. But it is important to remember to ask not only for changes in the outer world, but for your inner world to change as well. Remember, as one spiritual teacher put it, to "ask deeply." Ask for help to do what is right. Ask for new understanding. Ask to understand the meaning of your suffering. Ask for the courage to heal. Ask to know the deepest peace. Ask for the clarity to see behind the masks that we all wear to see the good and the holy in all people all the time. Ask that only the highest good be served in every situation. Ask to be used in the service of love.

> God help us to change. To change ourselves and to change our world. To know the need for it. To deal with the pain of it. To feel the joy of it. To undertake the journey without understanding the destination. Amen.
>
> from *The Prayer Tree* by Michael Luenig

> God grant me the serenity to accept the things I cannot change,
> The courage to change the things I can and
> The wisdom to know the difference.
>
> *The Serenity Prayer*

> Ask, and it shall be given you; seek and ye shall find; knock and it shall be opened unto you. Everyone that asketh receiveth; and he that seeketh findeth.
>
> from *The Bible:* Luke Chapter 11: 9-10 or Matthew 7: 7

PAUSE AND REFLECT

What are the things that you want at an outer level?
What are the things that you desire at an inner level?
Make a list. Allow yourself to ask.

Talking With God: Prayer can be an opportunity to sit down and have a good talk with your Higher Power. Get down and have a serious talk. Put some time aside. Open your heart to receive guidance. Let it be known that you are willing to change, and invite the spirit of a Higher Power to renew your life. Ask how to be a better person, a more loving husband, wife, friend, or parent. Ask how to live in the best way you are capable of living — with the most dignity and wisdom. Ask how to make the most out of your prison experience. Take time and get down to a real exchange and know that this inner work is more real than anything around you.

Imagine that someone who was totally wise and loving, someone who adores you and loves you is coming to visit you — would you refuse your visitor and watch television instead? This loving presence is there for you. Check it out. Take time to visit, tell all, ask questions, talk honestly, and listen very carefully.

PAUSE AND REFLECT

Within the next day set some time aside to pray. Have a talk with your Higher Power. If you don't believe there is such a Power, allow yourself to imagine yourself in a safe place meeting up with a very loving, compassionate, and wise being — perhaps a wise old man or woman. Imagine they are happy to see you. Imagine they are there to guide you and help you with any concerns that you have. Breathe deeply... Open to their great love and kindness. Share what is on your mind. Listen carefully for guidance. Imagine they are always there to help you. And know that the more you listen the more guidance you will receive.

Giving Thanks: With all the personal losses you face, with the pain you may be dealing with, with the negativity you confront every day, the idea of using prayer to give thanks may seem like a

bad joke at first. Maybe it is hard to think of things to be grateful
for. Yet a powerful way of praying and connecting with the spiritual
is to give thanks for those things that you do have. I remember reading the words of a saint once suggesting that the only prayer we ever
really needed to say was a prayer of gratitude. That alone would
change and uplift our life. As we give gratitude we lift ourselves up
above some of the darkness and acknowledge the rays of light in our
life. Offering thanks is a generous gesture on our part. It requires a
certain maturity and big-heartedness. Offering thanks is a way of
attracting grace into our life. We then find that there is more and
more to be grateful for.

PAUSE AND REFLECT

What do you have to be grateful for?
Make a list. Offer thanks.

Breath Prayer in the Heart: In addition to praying in particular
places or at certain times, (for example, in a chapel or before you go
to sleep), you might consider trying the powerful practice of prayer
called "breath-prayer in the heart." It is a way to bring prayer to your
entire day. When doing the breath-prayer, there is no distinction
between a time for prayer and a time for anything else. With this
approach even if you feel you have no time to pray, you can find
yourself praying at all times — with each breath you take. You
might choose a whole day or a part of a day and give it a try.

The directions are simple.

1. Choose a short breath-prayer. A breath-prayer is a spiritual
thought or phrase about three to six words long. It needs to be short
enough to be silently said in rhythm with one in-breath or out-
breath. It could be one thought or many thoughts, but each thought

should take no longer to repeat than the time it takes to naturally breath in or out.

2. As you repeat the breath-prayer, imagine breathing into your heart center. (The heart center is near your physical heart, but in the center of your chest. It is your spiritual heart.) Imagine the prayer is going in and out of your heart as you breathe.

The prayer could focus on love, healing, the name of a Spiritual Presence. It could be a thought from a prayer you are already familiar with or it could be one you create. Some examples are:

(on the in-breath)   Lord, make me an instrument
(on the out-breath)   of your peace
(Keep repeating while breathing in and out of the heart center)

(on the in-breath)   May all beings be peaceful
(on the out-breath)   May all beings be happy
(Keep repeating while breathing in and out of the heart center)

(on the out-breath)   May I know the power and goodness
(on the in-breath)   Of my own true nature
(Keep repeating while breathing in and out of the heart center)

3. Throughout your day, repeat the breath-prayer over and over to yourself in silence with the rhythm of your breathing. The breath-prayer, after you say it for awhile, goes to a sort of sub-conscious level and then you bring it back to mind when it comes to you. You might want to intentionally bring it to mind when you stand in line, walk around, or anywhere you desire.

Willie I often attend church services, and I pray every single morning upon arising. I pray for help for those I love and guidance for myself and I give thanks for all that He does for me. Whenever I have a conflict with a person or a situation and I feel myself getting angry or frustrated, I pray to God about it and then I let Him work through me. This always helps me find a positive solution to the conflict. Sometimes the answer comes to me through my own thoughts and sometimes it comes to me through something that somebody tells me. (I also talk about my problems to people whose opinions I trust). Sometimes I find the answer in something that I have read in the Bible that day. Either way, my prayers are always answered — not always as I expect them to be, but always in the way that I need.

Meditation

As mentioned in chapter ten, there are many kinds of meditation. Central to all meditation is focusing your attention and letting go of your usual thoughts. Meditation helps you develop the ability to quiet yourself enough to listen and trust what is often referred to as, the "still small voice within" — a voice of wisdom and compassion.

Meditation helps us learn to let go of our inner battles and to be present to all that is. Jack Kornfield, in his book, *A Path With Heart* wrote:

When we let go of our battles and open our heart to things as they are, then we come to rest in the present moment. This is the beginning and the end of spiritual practice. Only in this moment can we discover that which is timeless. Only here can we find the love that we seek. Love in the past is simply memory, and love in the future is fantasy. Only in the reality of the present can we love, can we awaken, can we find peace and understanding and connection with ourselves and the world.

If you have been doing the awareness meditation in chapter ten, you may wish to just stay with that practice. A few other forms of meditation are offered here. Whichever you choose, it is best to stick with one form. By doing this you will experience a deepening in the meditation that can only be achieved through regular practice.

Centering Prayer Meditation: Although this technique is called Centering "prayer," it is actually a meditation technique. I was introduced to this meditation through the work of a Catholic priest, Father Thomas Keating. In centering prayer the object of focus is what Father Keating refers to as "divine presence."

To do this meditation:

1. Get comfortable, close your eyes, take a few letting-go breaths.

2. Choose a "sacred word." It can be a word or name like peace, love, Jesus, Allah, trust, shalom, etc. This word is used as an anchor to the present and a pointer to inner stillness. Once you have chosen a word, silently repeat it, letting the repetition of the word coordinate with your breathing, as in the breath-prayer.

After you have focused on the sacred word in order to center yourself, gently let it go and then enter into the silence that is beyond words and sounds. Stay with this silence. When your mind wanders, as it naturally will, go back to the sacred word again. According to Father Keating, "you use the sacred word to remind yourself to let go of thoughts and return to the silence and dwell in the oneness of the Self."

The Relaxation Response: Another meditation technique is the Relaxation Response. In the Relaxation Response, you choose a word that could be a "sacred" word like the one chosen in the centering prayer, or a familiar word like the number "one," or you could choose a sound like "om." This word or sound is called a mantra. To do the Relaxation Response:

1. Find a comfortable position and take a few letting go breaths.

2. Then repeat your word or mantra with each breath.

3. When your mind wanders, gently bring your attention back to the repetition of the mantra again. Keep gently returning your attention to the mantra.

We experience the benefits of meditation best by meditating for at least twenty minutes a day. It is best to find a regular time so that the meditation practice becomes a part of your daily routine.

No matter what kind of meditation you do, your mind will wander into old patterns of thinking time and time again. You will, in all likelihood, find yourself judging yourself and questioning what you are doing. Whenever your mind wanders, wherever it wanders, just gently let go and come back to the moment, to the breath, to the sacred word, or to whatever the focus of your meditation. Studies have shown that even people who think they are not "getting anything out of the meditation" because their mind frequently wanders, still get significant benefit. They experience more self-control and less stress in their daily lives.

Remember, the mind wandering off into thoughts and feelings is a normal and unavoidable part of meditation. As many times as you find the mind wandering, gently, and without judgment, let go. Come back to the present moment. Your perseverance and patience will help you to move toward the deepest of healings — the realization that your inner peace is not dependent on outer circumstances, the realization that your inner power cannot be taken away by any person or situation, the realization that you are a spiritual being.

Basic Spiritual Truths

When you open to the spiritual, your load is always lightened. You increasingly clear the way for knowing — really knowing — certain basic spiritual truths about yourself. These basic spiritual truths are:

You are loved. This is the first spiritual truth, the most fundamental. The love I'm writing about here is not emotional, romantic, or superficial. When we go beyond the emotional and physical aspects of love to the spiritual, we realize it is something essential to life. As author, Robert Keck writes in his book, *Sacred Eyes*, "Love is the very core and essence of life.... It is not that we might *like* love to be central, or that we would *wish* it were more important. It is not that *if* we could design the perfect world we would put love at the center. The suggestion here is that love *is* the essential energy of the universe — we just haven't fully appreciated that fact."

You are worthy of respect and acceptance. Author Marianne Williamson writes, "We can't look to the world to restore our worth;.... It cannot crown us. Only God can crown us, and He already has... Do not look to the world for your sustenance or for your identity because you will not find them there." No matter how others feel toward you, "God adores you."

Your true nature is fundamentally good and beautiful. You are fundamentally good and beautiful even if your actions and some of the choices you've made haven't been.

You are needed in helping to heal the world. Healing one's self is helping to heal the world. The greatest responsibility that you have and the most important thing you can do is heal yourself and nurture your spiritual life. Get to know this lovable, loving and loved, valuable and valued, good and worthwhile Self. It is God's will that we become the magnificent beings we were created to be.

Willie It is my firm belief that one cannot say that one truly loves God unless one is willing to transform oneself for all time. To be "saved" is not to hand over responsibility, but to accept it completely. I can never again return to my previous life of drugs and crime, because I know clearly that I wll be cutting myself off from God. He has loved me even in my worst times and He has shown me mercy when I felt I didn't deserve it. But knowing that, really seeing that, makes me far more responsible now than I ever was in my previous state of ignorance. I know now that the only way to show my love for God on this earth is to show it through my treatment of others, and my respect for myself.

Spiritual Qualities

Praying, meditating, participating in religious services and rituals, and reading religious, spiritual, and inspirational books are some of the things we may "do." But we do them so that we can "live" from the best within us. The qualities that naturally arise from a commitment to our spiritual life, are those that make life more manageable, hopeful, and fulfilling.

Honesty: The idea of being honest applies not only to what you say but to the way you live. Honesty means you don't manipulate, bribe or project hidden agendas onto anyone or anything at anytime. When you live with honesty, you are not in conflict within yourself. And only then is inner peace really possible.

Trust and Faith: You may think of yourself as a person without faith, but, in truth, we are all people of faith. You put your faith in your ego or you put your faith in your Self and a higher power. You put your faith in denial or you put your faith in the willingness to see the truth. You put your faith in violent behavior or you put your faith in non-harming. You put your faith in fear or you put your faith in love.

As you grow spiritually, you mature in faith and in trust in yourSelf — trust that you can make good choices, trust that you can move your life in a positive direction. In addition, you grow in faith that there is much more to life than you had been aware of from the limited vantage point of the ego. You see there is a spiritual reality that supports and guides you, if you are willing to let it in. There is a growing faith that if you are open to it, you will be given what you need.

Even when outer circumstances seem insane, life takes on a much saner quality. You sense that there is a spiritual dimension to life and that you are an integral part of it.

Tolerance: With trust comes letting go of a need to judge yourself and others. Tolerance doesn't mean you let others walk all over you. It doesn't mean that you blind yourself to changes that you need to make or actions that you need to take. It means you are able to make them without aggression or hatred toward yourself or others. If you are strong in yourSelf, your need to manipulate or live in judgment of others fades away. If someone is different from you, you realize that you have had your own unique path to walk and out of a growing respect for your own life, you respect that others have their own path to walk as well.

Gentleness/Kindness: When you develop spiritually, you naturally become a more gentle, caring, and kind person. This does not mean you are or act like you are weak. Paradoxically, it is only the person who feels powerful who can afford to be kind and gentle. Rather than necessarily being one specific way of acting, gentleness is an inner state of mind. However, once you begin to trust this inner state, you find increasing discomfort with harming others. This discomfort comes from knowing that harming others, unless you are really in physical danger, is a dishonest act. Even in prison, you come to find greater strength in kindness. Although there may be times when you have to flex your muscles, you find more and more that you just don't need to play the game like you may have once thought you did.

Generosity: Generosity is an act of Self-expansion. In giving to someone else, you become greater. When you give something like love, kindness, or patience to another, by the very act of giving, you experience even more of it. Just think of times when you freely gave your love to someone. Didn't you have more love in your heart? Didn't you feel more love in your life? Think of a time when you freely gave some kindness to someone. Didn't you feel really good?

When you offered patience, did you feel more expansive and peaceful? When we think of generosity as a spiritual quality, we realize that *having rests on giving, not on getting.*

The more love you give, the more love you have. The more patience you offer, the more you feel the peace that you have extended to others. When giving is a wise and loving thing to do, even when you give away material things, you feel richer.

Patience: Although some people are naturally more patient than others, patience isn't so much something we are born with as something we cultivate. Meditation is a powerful tool for cultivating patience. When you are patient, time becomes your friend, instead of your enemy. Of course, you probably wish things would change in less time. But patience helps you to experience greater peace with the things you can't change for now. Patience helps you let go of your idea of how long things *should* take. It lets you feel more at ease with things as they are. Patience allows you to make the most of your time in prison (or anywhere else). Without it peace is impossible.

Forgiveness: As we've explored at length in earlier chapters, without forgiveness you are destined to be in conflict. Forgiveness allows you to stop dragging the past along with you. It is, without question, an essential key to peace, inner power, and freedom.

Justice: A person who has grown spiritually is committed to justice because, for one, true justice always promotes healing. Justice tries to take things that have been wronged and make them right.

In the case of criminal justice, true justice would promote healing by considering the real needs of both the offended and the offender. Anything less falls short of true justice-making. Injustice would be recognized and acknowledged. If a person has been harmed, his or her needs would be honored and attended to. Rather than just punishment for the offender, the goal would be restitution: the offender's acknowledgment of responsibility. This would include the offender's obligation to take steps of repayment for losses when possible. And there is the goal of reconciliation when possible. True justice holds the goal of recovery for everyone involved. With true justice, there is hope for the future. In his book on crime and justice, *Changing Lenses*, Howard Zehr writes," Redeeming love, not punishment, is the primary human responsibility."

Love: Being unaware of your heart's capacity to love and being unaware of your connection with The Divine, doesn't mean that they aren't there. It just means that you're not aware of them. At the heart of the spiritual is love. And it is love that ultimately heals, frees, and empowers us. When you get right down to it, every religious and spiritual teaching converges onto one path, and that is the path of the heart. Without heart, without increasing love and compassion for oneself and for others, all the rest is an empty form. Our inner spiritual core is love. And like the sun, it can be hidden by dark clouds, clouds of fear, negativity, and limiting beliefs. But it is never put out.

A Higher Purpose

Remember the story of the king who sends a person out to do a task. We're all on that mission. And we all seem to forget about the task we've been sent to accomplish while being distracted by other tasks. For example, you may have spent years developing a personality that easily attracts and impresses others; or you could use your time to sculpt a perfect body in the gym. Perhaps you worked hard to earn a college degree and can now speak for hours on a certain topic.

While all these accomplishments have value, if we aren't becoming more loving and offering love to others, the one task we're really sent into the world to do waits undone. When you get down to the bottom line, there is a higher purpose in life for you, for me, for all of us. This purpose is to bring the light of your spiritual Self into this beautiful, awesome, painful, and anguished world. The man who rules a corporate empire, affects or saves the lives of thousands by bringing them say needed medicine, but does it with greed in his heart may not meet his higher purpose. The prisoner who meets his or her fellow inmates with love and kindness does.

You have come here to be present and listen and respond to the voice and the call of your own heart. Then, regardless of the situation you find yourself in, you are a positive force, a healing presence.

As you align with your spiritual nature, when outer circumstances don't insure safety and people around you are difficult to deal with, you come to know an abiding inner safety and peace nonetheless. You become clearer and more powerful, finding your source of strength in a growing trust and faith in something infinitely greater than the sum of your small selves. There is the growing reliance on an aspect of your Self that includes, but is not bound by, the rational mind for direction and assurance.

The spiritual path opens the way for this awareness and for unexpected feelings. It offers the possibility that wherever you are, you can make it a battle ground or a sacred ground, more like heaven or more like hell.

The St. Francis Prayer
Lord make me an instrument
Of thy peace, where there is hatred, Let me sow love;
Where there is injury, pardon;
where there is doubt, faith;
Where there is despair, hope;
Where there is darkness, light;
And where there is sadness, joy.
O Divine Master, grant that
I may not so much seek
To be consoled as to console;
To be understood, as to understand;

To be loved as to love;
For it is in giving that we receive,
It is in pardoning that we
Are pardoned, and it is in dying
That we are born to eternal life.

CHAPTER 15

Wherever You Go, There You Are

YOU CAN'T MAKE the most of your life if you spend your time just planning ahead to some point in the future when you'll be out. Don't postpone living until you're released or until you have a job, have money or a lover by your side. Although life in prison can be incredibly challenging, if you use your time wisely there is a great pay-off. If you learn to develop greater insight and mental calm while inside, you'll be clearer, wiser, and more balanced (and therefore, much more in control) inside or outside — because *wherever you go, there you are!*

Even if you never get out, one thing is for sure, you'll always be with yourself. Regardless of your circumstances, your state of mind will always be the most important factor in determining how you feel and how effectively you deal with everyday encounters.

Taking It to the Streets

Although it isn't within the scope of this book to address the practical issues involved in making the move to life on the outside, I'd like to briefly address this issue here.

I recently spoke with Joe, a man who had participated in an Emotional Awareness Course a few years ago. Joe has now been out for a year. When I spoke with him he was doing really well. He has his own apartment. He is drug-free. He is enjoying life and hopeful about the future. He is working long hours at a job as a cook and has just finished a training program to manage the restaurant where he works. I asked Joe why he felt he was making such a positive go of life on the outside and what advice he would give to others. This was Joe's reply.

Joe When I went to prison I was tired of the lifestyle I had been living. I wanted to wipe my slate clean. I took advantage of the education and counseling programs. I found support in the prison and I planned to go to meetings and find support when I got out. I thought about what's going to go on for the rest of my life and I tried to plan everything I could plan for myself while I was in to make the best of getting out. I imagined my future in a positive way and started doing what I could to make it happen.

I think a lot of guys focus on their memories and look on them as good times even though they were bad times. A lot of guys think, "well I've got three to five years, so I'm going to sit here and be bored. I think a lot of guys generalize about the future and what they are going to do when they are out. They spend more time concentrating on the day they get out rather than trying to make a real plan for themselves. When they get out they party for a while and then they're lost again. They need to spend their time getting a better understanding of why they failed, rather than about the day they get out. They need to figure out who they are.

In order to hit the streets and stay on the streets, you have to prepare yourself while you're in and be committed to staying in touch with yourself regardless of the burdens that you have. In many ways being on the streets is no different than being in. You still have to deal with people who have attitudes. There's always going to be obstacles that slow you down from reaching goals as fast as you'd like. There's always going to be hardships. You have to learn to ACCEPT this as part of life. I notice that if people have turmoil in their life, they let that particular thing influence their entire life rather than seeing it as a part of their life. They let it take them over. In the past

I did the same thing. For instance, if I was in a relationship that didn't work out, that would affect everything else. It would interfere with my job and other parts of my personal life. I would let that situation emotionally and physically control me.

Today, I've learned to separate different aspects of my life and deal with them individually. This isn't easy and I still have instances of situations controlling me, but the biggest difference between dealing with these situations now than in the past is the fact that now I am aware of my reactions and am able to step back, look at myself, re-evaluate the situation, and move forward from there.

There's a saying in sports, "what you do in practice is what you do in the game." Prepare yourself now for the day you are released. Make a plan, set up a foundation for yourself, and practice self-awareness.

Joe offers some excellent advice. Let's take another look at what he has to say: Your best preparation for leaving is to use your time now to gain understanding into who you really are: Get understanding into the underlying reasons for why you are in prison. Use your time to develop self-awareness. Recognize that there is a part of you that is greater than your problems. Attend groups and get counseling when possible. Find a positive support system when you're out. Learn to recognize that most things in life are neither black nor white, but rather various shades of gray. Accept that obstacles are part of life. See yourself overcoming these obstacles and visualize a positive future. Even though few institutions offer counseling, vocational training, or practical preparation for release, try to make a practical plan in as much detail as possible for your transition to life on the outside.

By following Joe's advice you become more deeply rooted in your Self. Like a tree whose roots reach deeper and deeper into the earth for security and nourishment, you become stronger and more secure, discovering spiritual resources that can uplift and sustain you.

Then, when life's storms arise (and they will!) rather than becoming blown over or broken, you are able to bend with the wind and then rise up to stand tall again.

A Look Into Your Future

Take a few letting go breaths. Let yourself relax. Now imagine yourself five years from now. Take the time to get as clear a picture as you can.... What year is it? Where are you? What are you doing?

How are you feeling? Are you peaceful or angry? Are you feeling good about who you've become or are you feeling down on yourself? Are you feeling resentful and bitter or are you feeling forgiving and strong?

Do you spend some time caring for others or do you fill all your time sleeping, spacing out, being entertained, or thinking only of yourself? Do you take time to meditate, pray, and connect to the spiritual dimension of life? Or, do you spend all your time looking to others and the outside world for security and happiness?

What have you done with the last five years? As you look back, do you feel good about those five years?

* * *

Five years from now, whether you are still in prison or out on the streets, your answers to most of these questions will have been your choices. When you reflect back five years from now, will they have been years of anger and boredom? Or will they have been years of inner healing and positive change? Right now you are busy determining how you will answer these questions in five years. Your answers are going to be determined by how you choose to invest your energy NOW and how you choose to spend your time today and tomorrow. At least on an inner level you are in charge.

Don't wait for your partner, kids, cell-mate, or correctional officer to change. Don't wait for your jailer to let you out. The door to your inner life is always open. No counselor or clergy can make the changes for you. It's up to you.

Is This the End or the Beginning?

Even though you have come to the end of this book, I encourage you to read it over again from time to time as a reminder, guide, and inspiration. Let it serve to remind you that in each moment you can choose the way you relate to yourself, others, and the world around you. Let it serve as a guide to healing so that you can mend old wounds and come to know the power of awareness and love. Let it serve as an inspiration to keep growing. Rather than this just being the end of a book, I hope this is the beginning of a deeply healing and empowering journey for you. It is a journey that, if you are willing to take it, will last a lifetime. You just keep polishing yourself up more and more — so that today and tomorrow you can experience less conflict and confusion and greater peace, power, and freedom.

Prison, A Gift?

I end this book with a poem by Ralph, an inmate who attended the Emotional Awareness Course. Although the prison experience can be brutal for some, for Ralph, prison was a gift. It was a second chance at life. Prison gave him the opportunity to get off drugs and start to turn his life around.

Ralph

Prison, A Gift?
When all is lost you have a chance to start again anew.
What a gift indeed, to leave behind a life that was so blue.
A life of running from the pain, a pain that has no end.

What a gift in-need as you become your best and oldest friend.

Prison then is the Masters' way of calling you back home.

His gift is life, peace and hope, to heal your deepest wounds.

So you can accept this grace-full gift and rejoice with the angels
above,

Or turn again and run away and reject the Masters love.

My brothers, God is calling you. He has stripped you of foolish
pride.

He has taken all the worldly things behind which you could hide.

You have been forgiven. So give yourself a chance at life.

Give your heart a lift.

Know that God is with you, And prison is a gift.

ACKNOWLEDGMENTS

To BEGIN I want to express my great gratitude to the inmates who participated in the Emotional Awareness/Emotional Healing and the Psychology of Self courses that I have facilitated at the Massachusetts Correctional Institutions. A special thanks to the men at Baystate Correctional Center. Their courage, honesty, and deep commitment to personal growth have been a great inspiration.

My deepest gratitude goes to the men and women whose personal stories and insights bring important depth and life to each chapter of this book.

Special thanks to Joe Corbitt, Arnie King, Ed Lykus, and Hector Rodriguez for their enthusiastic encouragement and willingness to offer important feedback on the first draft.

Many, many thanks to the key editors: to Jan Johnson for her astute editorial input; to Betsy West for her great generosity and insightful and creative feedback; and to Naomi Raiselle whose support and creative input has always made a significant difference in the work I bring to the public.

A very special thanks to Toni Burbank of Bantam Books. Toni was editor of my first book, *Forgiveness: A Bold Choice for A Peaceful Heart*. The creative suggestions and expertise she offered in my first book filter throughout the pages of *Houses of Healing*.

Many thanks to Dr. Craig Love, Dr. Julia Hall and Ian Tink for their thoughtful comments on the original manuscript.

Thank you to former prison counselors Pat Butner and Marcelino

DeLeon who set me off into the journey of teaching in the prison setting. I am eternally grateful to both of you.

My heartfelt thanks to Impress, Inc. (Northampton, MA) and especially to Dan Mishkind for his great generosity and patience. Dan's skillful and creative graphic talents have been an enormous gift to me and this project.

Many thanks go to the board of directors of the Lionheart Foundation who continually support and encourage this work. Thank you Ilene Robinson, Sally Jackson, Andrew Silver, Justin Freed, Suzanne Roger, and Joan Borysenko.

A heartfelt thanks go to the many people who have contributed to the Lionheart Foundation over the past few years. They have helped to make the Lionheart Prison Project possible.

My deepest thanks go to many wonderful friends who are a constant source of encouragement and love. Among them are Peggy Taylor who encouraged me to start the Lionheart Foundation. Fella Cederbaum who has supported this work in numerous ways; Dot Walsh whose commitment to teaching peace and justice is an ongoing inspiration.

Without the vision and extraordinary support of Celia Hubbard, Ryah, and Drs. Joan and Mirren Borysenko this book would not have materialized. Thank you ever so much.

I am eternally grateful that I have been given the great grace and blessing to teach and learn from the men and women who have attended the "Emotional Awareness" and "Psychology of Self" courses.

REFERENCES

INTRODUCTION

Bo Lozoff. *We're All Doing Time.* Human Kindness Foundation. 1985. (Prison-Ashram Project Rt. 1 Box 201-N Durham, NC 27705)

CHAPTER THREE

Lucia Capacchione. *Recovery of Your Inner Child.* New York: Simon and Schuster/ Fireside, 1991.

John Bradshaw. *Homecoming: Reclaiming and Championing Your Inner Child.* New York: Bantam, 1990.

CHAPTER FOUR

John Bradshaw. *Homecoming: Reclaiming and Championing Your Inner Child.* New York: Bantam, 1990.

CHAPTER SIX

William Worden. *Grief Counseling and Grief Therapy: A Handbook for the Mental Health Practitioner.* New York: Springer Publishing Co., 1982.

Clarissa Pinkola Estes. *Women Who Run With the Wolves.* New York: Ballantine Books, 1992.

Judy Tatelbaum. *The Courage to Grieve.* New York: Harper Row, 1984.

REFERENCES

CHAPTER SEVEN

Gerald Jampolsky. *Good-bye to Guilt: Releasing Fear Through Forgiveness.* New York: Bantam, 1985.

CHAPTER NINE

Joan Borysenko. *Minding the Body. Mending the Mind.* New York: Bantam, 1988.

CHAPTER TEN

Jon Kabat-Zinn. *Full Catrastrophe Living.* New York: Delacorte Press, 1990.

Thomas Keating. *Open Mind, Open Heart.* Warwick, New York: Amity House, 1986.

Jack Kornfield. *A Path With Heart.* New York: Bantam, 1993.

Joan Borysenko. *Fire In The Soul.* New York: Warner, 1993.

CHAPTER ELEVEN

Howard Zehr. *Changing Lenses: A New Focus on Crime and Justice.* Scottdale, Pennsylvania: Herald Press, 1990.

Ramond Moody. *Life After Life.* New York: Bantam, 1976.

———. *Reflections on Life After Life.* New York: Bantam, 1978.

———.*The Light Beyond.* New York: Bantam, 1989.

CHAPTER TWELVE

Hugh Prather. *Notes on How to Live in the World and Still Be Happy.* New York: Doubleday, 1986.

CHAPTER THIRTEEN

Terry Dobson. "A Kind Word Turneth Away Wrath." © 1981 by Terry Doson. Reprinted by permission of the author.

A Course in Miracles. Farmington, New York: The Foundation for Inner Peace, 1975.

CHAPTER FOURTEEN

Paul Tillich. "To Whom Much Was Forgiven." *Parabola: The Magazine of Myth and Tradition.* Volume XII, number 3, 1987.

Sogyal Rinpoche. *The Tibetan Book of Living and Dying.* New York: Harper San Francisco, 1992.

Robert Keck. *Sacred Eyes.* Indianapolis, Indiana: Knowledge Systems, Inc. 1992.

Micheal Leunig. *The Prayer Tree.* Victoria, Australia: Collins Dove (a division of Harper Collins), 1991.

The Bible

Jack Kornfield. *A Path With Heart.* New York: Bantam, 1993.

Marianne Williamson. *A Woman's Worth.* New York: Random House, 1993.

Thomas Keating. *Open Mind, Open Heart.* Warwick, New York: Amity House, 1986.

Howard Zehr. *Changing Lenses: A New Focus on Crime and Justice.* Scottdale, Pennsylvania: Herald Press, 1990.

ORDERING INFORMATION

Houses of Healing: A Prisoner's Guide to Inner Power and Freedom can be ordered through the Lionheart Foundation.

If you are incarcerated and want to purchase a personal copy of *Houses of Healing*, send $8 (includes postage and handling) to the Lionheart Foundation.

Individual copies for anyone who is not incarcerated:

$12 plus $3 s&h total $15
Canadian orders: $16 plus $4 s&h total $20

Bulk rates for orders of 10 books or more: $10 each postpaid
Bulk rates for Canadian orders: $13 each postpaid

For orders from outside of the U.S. and Canada please send only checks drawn on a U.S. bank in U.S. dollars, or an international postal money order in U.S. dollars.

Please make all payments by check or money order to:

The Lionheart Foundation
Box 194 Back Bay
Boston, MA 02117

For prison counseling staffs, clergy, and volunteers: A *Houses of Healing* training manual with guidance and suggestions for facilitating groups based on *Houses of Healing* can be ordered through the Lionheart Foundation. $20 plus $3 s&h.

ABOUT THE AUTHOR

FOR THE PAST fifteen years author, counselor, and educator, Robin Casarjian, M.A., has been sharing her perspectives on emotional healing with people from all walks of life. Whether working in inner city classrooms, hospitals, corporations or prisons, Robin's work has been widely acclaimed for its clarity, directness, and unwavering vision of the enormous potential within all people. Her first book, *Forgiveness: A Bold Choice for A Peaceful Heart* was published by Bantam Books in 1992.

Since 1988 Robin's work has focused on offering courses called "Emotional Awareness/Emotional Healing" to incarcerated men and women. The depth, scope and power of her transformative message has brought inspiration, hope, and healing to hundreds of inmates. Now in *Houses of Healing: A Prisoner's Guide to Inner Power and Freedom*, Robin shares her work for all to benefit from.

In order to broaden the scope of her prison work Robin established the Lionheart Foundation. Lionheart's goal is to place multiple copies of *Houses of Healing* in every prison library in America — offering all who are emotionally imprisoned a guide to finding personal freedom, inner power, and greater peace of mind.